Practical
Academic

THESIS BY PUBLICATION

Effectively develop and deliver a well-structured compilation thesis

Jennifer Rowland

Practical Academic. Thesis by Publication

Copyright © 2017 by Jennifer Rowland

All rights reserved.

No part of this book may be used or reproduced in any manner whatsoever without written permission except in the case of brief quotations embodied in critical articles or reviews.

This publication is designed to provide information to promote thought on delivering a thesis by publication, or compilation thesis. It is sold with the understanding that the writer and publisher are not engaged in rendering legal, business, accounting, or other professional advice. If legal advice or other expert assistance is required, the services of a competent professional should be sought. This book presents examples and concepts related to activities involved in organizing the structure and content of a thesis by publication. It has intentionally been written in a way to omit any specific names, characters, places, or incidents. The intention is to reinforce concepts and various approaches by considering how they might be employed in the presentation of the work. Any mistakes in this reflective work are made by the author and not the experts who generously provided their time to provide information.

For information contact Jennifer Rowland
http://www.practicalacademic.com

Book cover design by Bek Pickard from Zebedee Design.

ISBN-10: 0-6481070-0-0
ISBN-13: 978-0-6481070-0-2

First Edition: June 2017
10 9 8 7 6 5 4 3 2 1

Foreword

Thank you so much for buying this book!

    Having worked as an academic editor and consultant for a number of years, I routinely consulted and supported students through the delivery of their thesis by publication. I soon realized that few resources are available to guide students through the requirements, which can be incredibly diverse depending on the institution with which they are affiliated. Nonetheless, there are some central components of delivering a thesis by publication that appear to be common between the institutional guidelines.

    The purpose of this guide is to give you a quick reference to aid you in the development of your thesis by publication. I cover the basic considerations in your project development and publication delivery, and the importance of creating a cohesive narrative that delivers a holistic study, rather than dispersed, unrelated investigations. I share some tips on elegant approaches that you might consider including in the presentation of your work.

    The eight chapters of this book follow the delivery of the thesis, including: planning, outlining, structuring, and delivering your manuscript. I discuss each major section in order, from start to finish, and I have shared tips and examples to help you understand the type of content that you might incorporate in your work. **Exercises** are included at the end of chapters to relate the concepts to your own experiences. **Some downloadable materials** are listed at the end of chapters. Those materials can be accessed from my companion website (www.practicalacademic.com/resources).

    This book is mostly a practical guide, focused on helping you to deliver a quality dissertation with a clean, clear structure that will prove easy for your examiners and peers to comprehend. I sincerely hope that the materials presented here can help you to successfully prepare your thesis by publication. I welcome you to this first edition and look forward to reading your feedback, because I am always looking to improve my work.

With warm regards,
Jennifer Rowland

Table of Contents

Disclaimer and Acknowledgements 5

SUMMARY OF CHAPTERS 7

CHAPTER 1: Planning Your PhD 8

CHAPTER 2: Practical Preparation 25

CHAPTER 3: Preliminary Pages 35

CHAPTER 4: Introduction, Literature Review, and Aims 56

CHAPTER 5: A Word on Methods 66

CHAPTER 6: Results/Papers Chapters 72

CHAPTER 7: Discussion, References, and Appendices 88

CHAPTER 8: Tying it all Together 98

SUMMARY 115

Disclaimer

The material and opinions presented in this book are my own and not representative of any other party or organization.

Acknowledgements

This book would not be a reality without many years of experience working with the excellent staff at Helsinki University Language Services, in particular Leena Evesti and Outi Ala-Kahrakuusi. Thank you both so much. Once again, thanks also to the ongoing encouragement and support of Guy and Michaela Windsor. For sharing their critical eye, I am immensely grateful to Rosa Didonna, Catarina Vila Pouca, Wai Kuen Chow, and Tesha Tsai. Huge thanks to Becca Judd who has provided outstanding proofreading of the manuscript, and Bek Pickard who designed the cover. My beautiful children Rafael and Maya have been incredibly understanding and supportive during the creation of this book, for which I am immensely grateful. To my friends and family, thank you so much for your incredible support, it means the world to me.

Glossary

For the purposes of this book, the following terminologies are employed.

Combination Thesis/Mixed Thesis: a thesis presenting novel findings in both publication and traditional format, depending on chapter.

Conference Proceeding: body of work presented to a conference, typically in a paper format, and published as a collection of proceedings. More substantial than a conference abstract.

Dissertation/Thesis: document delivered for assessment as a requirement to be awarded a doctoral degree.

Essay Thesis: a thesis study presented as a collection of unpublished independent essays.

Publication/Journal Article/Paper: an academic report published in an academic journal after peer review by one or more referees.

State of the Art: represents the current state of advancement and/or knowledge in the field, including the newest and most recent ideas and methods.

Thesis by Chapters/Traditional Thesis/Monograph Thesis: a thesis/dissertation where original methods and results are delivered in chapters.

Thesis by Publication/Compilation Thesis/Article Thesis: a thesis study where the results chapters are presented as journal articles/publications.

SUMMARY OF CHAPTERS

In this book, I introduce and discuss the key concepts that encompass the delivery of a thesis by publication, or a compilation thesis for a doctoral degree. Throughout the following chapters, I break down the components of each section and discuss the type of content that you should include. I also review issues relating to presentation and structure. This discussion is presented in the following chapters:

- **Chapter 1** introduces some key planning considerations for when you are commencing your doctoral studies.
- **Chapter 2** outlines the overall structure and set-up for your dissertation.
- **Chapter 3** describes the content that can be included in the preliminary pages of your thesis.
- **Chapter 4** discusses the delivery of your introduction, literature review, and aims.
- **Chapter 5** overviews the way in which you may include a "methods" section in your thesis.
- **Chapter 6** overviews the sections that present the publications/results that you are demonstrating for your thesis.
- **Chapter 7** focuses on the discussion, references, and appendices.
- **Chapter 8** summarizes the activities required to complete and deliver the final manuscript.

This guide is delivered from the point of view of aiding a student who is aiming to deliver a thesis by publication at an academic research institution or university. The principal type of research discussed throughout this book is assumed to be experimentally-focused, predominantly quantitative, and pursuing hypothesis-testing investigations. Nonetheless, those pursuing alternative investigation styles may still benefit from the concepts discussed here.

CHAPTER 1

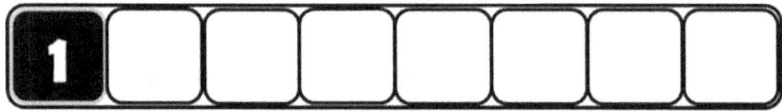

Planning Your PhD

Competition in the academic research sector is constantly expanding, with ever more graduates vying for a diminishing funding pot. Young researchers need more than ever to develop their profile. Whilst traditional theses continue to serve many doctoral graduates, thesis by publication represents an approach that forces the student and their mentor to consider practical output within the timeframe of the doctoral work. This can boost both professional profiles: that of the supervisor/mentor, and that of the student pursuing the research.

Pursuing a thesis by publication should be coupled with solid project management strategies that focus on delivering a set number of research publications: typically 2–8 within one body of work. This approach mirrors the expected professional practice that should be taken during even briefer postdoctoral training, which should enable the junior researcher to be able to develop their own research profile within only a few short years. For simplicity, here we will focus on a standard 3-year full-time doctoral study.

Project Planning

Many issues have come about with students taking far too long to complete their theses. Oftentimes this is due to supervisors outlining **overly ambitious projects** that will certainly result in a raised profile for the group and those involved, but which have a high chance of failure. Strategic project planning is absolutely essential to maximize outcomes within the timeframe of the work.

Developing a Project/Publication Plan

In order to deliver a thesis by publication, you should develop a solid plan at the beginning of your doctoral studies to determine the anticipated projects that you will pursue. You can refine and adapt such a project timeframe as the project progresses. Working together with your research supervisor, you should **establish a clear schedule** for how you think the research will progress over the entire course of your thesis. This will most likely change as you actively pursue the work and confront stumbling blocks along the way (if it was easy, everyone would do it, right?); but having the basic plan from which to begin is a starting point, and it helps you to keep track and reorganize your project clearly when you need to adapt to changes in the work. This exercise also helps you to get on the same page when it comes to goal setting with your supervisor. You might deliver this type of planning in a number of ways. You might include all these in a dossier for your research planning at the commencement of your doctoral studies.

Approaches to project planning

1: List format

You and your supervisors should be able to develop a list of all of the research goals for the doctoral studies that you aim to pursue. As such, you can list the major goals or research questions that you will pursue, and the expected outcomes.

2: Major foci and microdeliverables

You may choose to take a systematic approach and split up the outcomes from your research into major goals and microdeliverables, or steps, that you need to achieve in order to reach your major goals.

3: GANNT chart (goals/activities over time)

The preparation of a GANNT chart to structure your research goals into a timeline can help you to obtain a broad overview that highlights issues (e.g. table 1.1). Creating this type of project plan can clarify where you have overburdened your time, and help you to identify where you can include contingency time to address issues that you may need to troubleshoot in your work.

4: Report

You might choose to incorporate all of these formats into a collated report where you outline the entire project plan in great detail, fully referenced. Many institutions request this at the commencement of a doctoral study, and this approach aligns well when funding was recently secured for, or is sought for, the project.

Creating a timeframe and project plan can help to determine how your thesis will develop over the course of the 3-year PhD. In turn, you can create a **plan for your thesis publications** at the outset, which can serve as a blueprint that you work from as you progress with your work. By no means does this imply that your project cannot change when required, and in some cases projects need to be completely discontinued for various reasons. However, this provides an essential structure that can be constantly revised and kept up to date to ensure that, as you progress, you are considering what you are going to deliver at the end of your PhD.

CHAPTER 1: Planning your PhD

Table 1.1: GANNT chart for three year project

Task	1	2	3	4	5	6	7	8	9	10	11	12	13	14	15	16	17	18	19	20	21	22	23	24	25	26	27	28	29	30	31	32	33	34	35	36
PROJECT 1																																				
Literature review	■	■	■	■	■	■	■	■	■	■																										
Set up / ordering		■	■	■																																
Harvesting samples			■	■	■	■	■																													
Analysis — method 1							■	■	■	■																										
Analysis — method 2								■	■	■																										
Draft paper										■	■																									
Publication 1												■																								
PROJECT 2																																				
Literature review						■	■	■	■	■	■	■	■	■	■	■	■	■	■																	
Set up / ordering							■	■	■																											
In vitro studies								■	■	■	■	■	■	■	■																					
Implantation studies															■	■	■	■	■	■	■															
Publication 2 and 3																			■	■	■	■														
PROJECT 3																																				
Set up / ordering							■	■	■	■																										
Cell culture												■	■	■	■																					
In vivo investigation												■	■	■	■	■	■	■	■	■	■	■	■	■												
Microarray																								■	■	■	■									
Northern/Western																										■	■	■								
Publication 4 and 5																											■	■	■	■						
Thesis preparation																												■	■	■	■	■	■	■	■	■

SMART Planning

When designing a project, it is wise to consider how you will gauge its success. The measures of project success should be clear to the project team, and to those funding the work. The SMART method is a popular approach for determining what success means to a project (Doran, 1981).

Specific
Measurable
Attainable
Realistic
Timely

The SMART criteria can be applied to the academic research project to frame the value of the project that you are designing. The five main steps are outlined here in order.

Specific — you need to incorporate specific goals into your project, outlining achievable deliverables.

Measurable — determine clear, measurable waypoints and outcomes that represent goal attainment.

Attainable — make a clear outline of how the defined goals and deliverables can be practically achieved.

Realistic — ensure the goals you are working toward are those you are willing and able to pursue.

Timely — the goals you are aiming for must be achievable within the timeframe that you have outlined. Clear timelines must be set.

Taking the SMART criteria into consideration when you are preparing a project plan is helpful to ensure that you are designing your project well.

PLANNING HELPS TO

- **strategize together with your supervisor;**
- **plan the expected publications;**
- **pre-empt any issues that may arise; and**
- **draft a framework for your thesis that you can adapt as you go along.**

When planning out your doctoral studies, it is important to consider how the investigations are going to link together to create one "body of work." Doctoral students are easily swayed and sometimes can come to the end of their research training with several very good but completely unrelated publications. When you sit down to plan, ensure that your research publications build a cohesive narrative. This is simply demonstrated in figure 1.1. Each paper should naturally lead to the next to create a logical study progression.

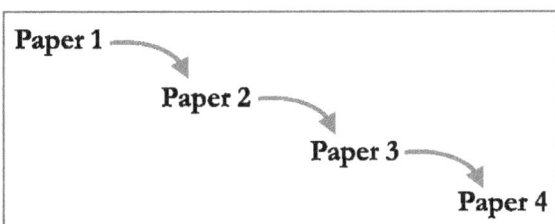

Figure 1.1: Classical study flow for thesis by publication results chapters.

Establishing Your Relationship With Your Supervisor

One of the key management issues you need to plan for your doctoral studies is the establishment of a clear working relationship with your supervisor(s). Your doctoral studies will run far more smoothly if there is clarity regarding expectations from all parties. I advocate that you consider preparing a **mentoring agreement** at the commencement of your doctoral studies. In this agreement you should both agree and *sign off* on what you, the doctoral candidate, pledge to deliver (table 1.2). This reassures both parties and renders accountability in the process. Most importantly, your supervisor must commit to supporting you, the doctoral student, in the advancement of your research and professional development as you pursue your investigation(s). Some of the key points that you might incorporate in a mentoring agreement include the following.

Meetings schedule
Clarify how often and for what duration you are required to attend and participate in meetings. These might be related to your group, to a resource that you utilize in your work, or to other activities related to your doctoral work.

Hours of work
How many hours each week are you expected to work during your candidature, and which hours of the day? Are you going to be performing field work or data collection at odd hours? Will you be expected to travel; if so, when and how much? These are expectations and requirements that should be established at the commencement of your candidature.

Table 1.2: Mentoring checklist

A mentoring checklist like this could be completed by you and your supervisor at the beginning of your doctoral studies. You should both keep a copy for future reference.

Mentoring agreement checklist	
Duration of mentoring arrangement.	
Purpose of mentoring arrangement.	
How often will we meet?	
What style will those meetings be? (Formal presentation, informal chat, coffee break; meeting duration, at least once every X weeks.)	
The role of the mentor is:	
The role of the mentee is:	
Our meetings will be confidential/not confidential.	
The mentor will provide honest and constructive advice regarding the mentee's work and progress.	AGREE or DISAGREE
The mentee will acknowledge the advice and take it into consideration in their research pursuits when actively pursuing their investigation.	AGREE or DISAGREE
The mentor agrees to provide feedback regarding written materials being published during the period of the mentoring arrangement.	AGREE or DISAGREE
The mentor agrees to promote progression of the mentee's work, wherever and whenever possible.	AGREE or DISAGREE
Authorships arising from the work will include the mentor as final author and mentee as first author, unless otherwise agreed upon.	AGREE or DISAGREE — CLARIFY
Training will be provided regarding: equipment, experimental approaches, project management, academic writing, conference presentation, other … (may relate to departmental requirements).	Specify training here.
Signatures: (Date and printed name)	

Financial support
What kind of scholarship and research financial support do you have for completing your doctoral research? Will it carry the whole project? Do you have any contingency? Do you have a travel budget? This is the type of information you need to source at the commencement of your studies to be able to proactively budget.

Attendance (to institutional seminars or other activities)
What institutional seminars or activities will you be expended to attend or participate in during your candidature?

Conference attendance (abstracts/papers)
You have much to gain from presenting your work to a wider audience. Benefits might include networking, acquiring resources or ideas, and identifying potential groups you might work with in the future. It is wise to agree on expectations regarding conference presentation (international/national/abstract/proceeding) and which work you might be able to offer in this regard from your planned research project.

Expected deadlines and deliverables
In line with the project planning that you need to do prior to commencing your practical work (*vide infra*), you should agree with your supervisor regarding your expected deadlines and deliverables.

Support provided (resources, technical, or collaborative)
What kind of support is available to you as a research student should be determined at the outset so that you have an awareness of what resources are available as you proceed. I recommend creating a spreadsheet of these resources. This might pertain to resources, technical support, or collaborative support related to your work. See table 1.3 for an example.

Table 1.3: Institutional Resources

	INSTITUTIONAL SERVICES AVAILABLE				
	Mouse Biology, Myopathy and Therapeutics				
TYPE OF SERVICE	**DETAIL OF SERVICE**	**LOCATION**	**CONTACT**	**LINKED STAFF**	**COST**
Computing	Provide IT support, programs, hardware/software, installations	Biology Department IT, Room 365	Service Desk, ext. 5468, IT@bio.uni.edu	Approval from X Marques for service over $100	Invoiced case-by-case
Learning support	Provide assistance with design of courses and Moodle delivery	Uni Learning Center, Room 12	Service Desk, ext. 5490, LS@uni.edu	Postgraduates and staff may consult at any time	Free
Counseling	Personal counseling for all staff and students	Uni Welfare Center, ground floor	UWC, ext. 5423, UWC@uni.edu	Students and staff receive eight free consults per year.	Free
Grant applications	Research grant application support, re: guidelines, structure, review	Research Office, building 5, room 341	RO, ext. 5434, RO@uni.edu	X Marques access	Free
Statistics	Statistical advice and analysis where required	Statistics Office, Math Department	Stats Office, ext. 5410, Stats@math.uni.edu	Postdoctoral and staff may set up consultancy	Consultation free, analysis invoiced case-by-case
Printing	Printing posters, theses, and large manuals, and photocopying service	University Printery, Central Services District	Uni Printery, ext. 5472, Uniprint@uni.edu	Accessible to everyone	Students = 10% discount, invoiced case-by-case
Equipment	Advice regarding locating and accessing various equipment on campus	Faculty Manager, G48, Building 8	John Jones, ext. 5443 BioManage@uni.edu	Accessible to everyone	Free
Editing/Revision	Document language revision to perfect English standard	Language Services, Central Services District	Joanna Briggs, ext. 5436, languageservice@uni.edu	Accessible to everyone	Research students 15% discount, invoiced case-by-case

<u>Potential inclusions to database of resources</u>

- Computing services
- Outreach and communication
- Contracts and HR
- Departmental services
- Secretary
- Administrators
- Core facilities
- Postgraduate conveners
- Counseling services
- Accounting
- Learning and teaching
- Available equipment
- Careers services
- Mentoring network
- Staff and postgraduate clubs
- Office of research integrity
- Postgraduate studies office
- Statistical support
- Printing services

<u>Record keeping</u>
You need to decide upon — and discuss with your supervisor — the best practice in record keeping as you launch into your studies. There may be established practice in your group, or you may wish to employ new and/or innovative approaches. In any case, your supervisor needs to be aware of the practices that you are following, and you need to be aware of what their expectation is for your record keeping.

<u>Ownership of the work</u>
Whether or not you will be able to pursue the work beyond your doctoral studies should be discussed at the beginning of your PhD. This is particularly important for students pursuing work that will yield intellectual property that might be commercialized later. You should be proactive in clarifying your ownership of innovation that may be potentially lucrative for you in the long run.

Other work
You need to discuss with your supervisor if you are participating in other work during your doctoral studies. Many, if not most, doctoral students will participate in teaching or tutoring in their university, which aids ongoing professional development. You might have a night or weekend job, and most institutions require that you disclose this when you commence doctoral studies.

Target Journals
If you anticipate delivering a thesis by publication, you should certainly create a list of the preferred target journals that your research focus may be suitable for. This will allow you to research the style of presentation, how rigorous the data analysis should be, and time required for publication. It is important for your scheduling to gauge how long each target journal will take to evaluate and publish your paper. You are on a tight deadline during your doctoral studies, so you may choose to publish with a journal that reviews more rapidly and offers more issues per year.

END OF CHAPTER 1 SUMMARY
Planning the Thesis by Publication

Here I have discussed some basic considerations regarding planning for your doctoral studies that will ultimately result in the submission of a thesis by publication. The key topics covered include:

- Develop a publication and project plan from the outset that you can modify as you pursue your investigation.

- Be SMART about creating a project plan at the start of your studies.

- Be proactive in defining your supervisor/student relationship and expectations at the outset.

- Clarify and record the available resources and support, as well as required deadlines impacting your candidature.

EXERCISE 1.1: INSTITUTIONAL SERVICES
Create a summary of the institutional services available to you as a research student. Include details of how you can access them and any conditions relating to their use.

Exercise 1.1: Institutional Resources

INSTITUTIONAL SERVICES AVAILABLE

TYPE OF SERVICE	DETAIL OF SERVICE	LOCATION	CONTACT	LINKED STAFF	COST

EXERCISE 1.2: MAP YOUR DISSERTATION

Create a map of how your study will flow from publication to publication, considering figure 1.1.

EXERCISE 1.3: GANNT YOUR DOCTORAL PLAN

Create a GANNT chart to outline the timeline for your studies, anticipating the work and how it will be completed within your doctoral training period. Use the template provided on the next page, which may be downloaded from www.practicalacademic.com.

CHAPTER 1: Planning your PhD

GANNT chart for three year project

36													
35													
34													
33													
32													
31													
30													
29													
28													
27													
26													
25													
24													
23													
22													
21													
20													
19													
18													
17													
16													
15													
14													
13													
12													
11													
10													
9													
8													
7													
6													
5													
4													
3													
2													
1													

Thesis preparation

Chapter 1 – Downloadable Materials
Download from www.practicalacademic.com

- Exercise 1.3/Table 1.1: "GANNT overview" – Excel file containing a blank template and an example provided in chapter 1.
- Table 1.2: "Mentoring checklist" – Word file containing a template.
- Exercise 1.1/Table 1.3: "Institutional resources" – Excel file containing a blank template and the example provided in chapter 1.

References — chapter 1

Doran, G.T. (1981). "There's a S.M.A.R.T. way to write managements' goals and objectives." Management Review. AMA FORUM. 70(11):35-36.

CHAPTER 2

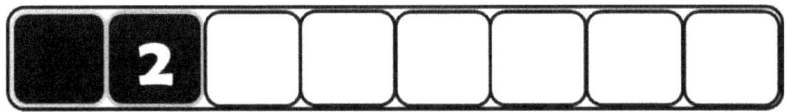

Practical Preparation

Now that we have discussed the planning of your thesis by publication, let us cover some practical considerations. Here I introduce the main sections that you may include to your dissertation, major formatting concerns, and other key issues you need to address in order to be able to deliver the work.

Laying Out Your Manuscript

Once you have your project plan in place and the work is underway, you can start to think about how your actual thesis will look. Most doctoral students will wait until most or all of their papers are completed or published before beginning this activity; however, I would encourage you to start early.

When setting up your template layout for your thesis by publication, the overall structure usually incorporates a number of sections that support the delivery of a research investigation spanning multiple publications that are connected by an overriding theme. These include the following, which can be used as section headers:

Prepages

- Title page.
- Statement of originality.
- Table of contents.
- List of tables.
- List of figures.
- List of original publications.
- List of contributors.

- Acknowledgements.
- Abstract/Summary.

<u>Main body of work</u>
- Introduction.
- Literature review.
- Aims of study.
- Chapters of research papers.
- Conclusions, summary, and future directions.
- References/Bibliography.
- Appendices.

How these sections are put together will vary from thesis to thesis, and institutions can set individual guidelines regarding their expectations for structure and content. When planning how to draft your thesis, you should consider these sections in more detail, and how you might address them. What exactly goes into each section? I will be covering that in following chapters. Similarly, the number of chapters that you include in your thesis will vary according to the individual papers that you are presenting. I will talk more about the types of publications that you can include in your thesis in chapter 3. For now, creating headings in your manuscript for these sections is a great start towards preparing your thesis.

Thesis Formatting Issues
When you first sit down to set up your thesis manuscript, you need to consider the formatting issues that should be standardized for your thesis. This can prove challenging because the individual papers will adhere to various style guides that may not match. Paper I may be delivered in American English and Paper II in British; some may use Vancouver style, and another, Chicago. When you write for publication (chapter 6), you must write in a targeted style for your target journal. For the sections that surround the research papers, you need to

standardize your style. **Choose one style and standardize this for the thesis manuscript surrounding the publications.** Here is a handy list of things you should consider when standardizing your layout and formatting.

Language: Are you using American (US) or British (UK) English? It is possible that you have papers in the thesis that use both. Select your preference for the surrounding manuscript and stick to that style. No change is required for the language of the journal articles.

Oxford comma: Are you using the Oxford comma, or not? Yes or no, standardize throughout.

Numerics: Are you counting from one to ten, or one to nine, or 1–10 and 1–9? Do you count people with numerics (1, 2, … 10, 11) or written numbers (one, two, … ten, eleven)? What about sample numbers?

Page and section numbers: You need to consider the style of page and section numbers that you will utilize in your thesis manuscript. These will be discussed further in later sections. Common styles are noted here:

- Prepages numbered i, ii, iii, iv …
- Pages numbered 1, 2, 3, 4 …
- Sections numbered 1, 1.1, 1.1.1, 2, 2.1, 2.1.1, 3 …
- Papers numbered I, II, III, IV …

Spacing: Do you need to use single-spaced, double-spaced, or 1.5-spaced text in your thesis? Check your institution's guidelines. Similarly, do you include spaces or indentation between paragraphs, or around headings and captions?

Margins: You need to check your institution's instructions on how to layout your thesis. Set this up early to minimize the drama of having to reformat your thesis at the last minute. You need to determine the page size and margins; also, are they mirrored or regular?

Font: What type and size of font will you be using throughout your thesis? Does your institution provide a guideline for that? What format will your headings use? Are you using captions, and what do they look like?

Referencing: What style will you be using for your referencing? Will you use referencing software? Will you use a single reference section at the end of the thesis or will you use footnotes? (This is often discipline-specific.) Will you employ Vancouver or Harvard style? (Chapter 7.)

Practical Concerns
You should prepare for other practical concerns surrounding the delivery of a thesis by publication . Several main issues are discussed below.

Printing and binding
It might feel like a long way away, but getting an idea of where and how you will eventually print and bind your thesis can save you a lot of stress if you identify your options at the beginning of your doctoral journey. Consider discussing the practicalities with the printer, and find out early how payment for the services works. Avoid last-minute dashes for printing, which would inevitably end in stress and, typically, errors in your thesis printing.

Digital thesis collections
Universities are now embracing the creation of digital thesis collections internationally, which means that your thesis is going to reach a wider audience after you complete your doctoral studies. As such, you should be very clear on the requirements for your digital thesis manuscript.

Examiner selection

You will probably not select your examiner until about six months prior to handing in your thesis, but it is good to be clear on what your institution's guidelines are for examiner selection. How many do you need? Do they have to be external or can they be internal to your institution? Establish your requirements early, so you can take some time to consider as you progress in your research.

Time for examination

For several reasons, it is important to identify how long examination will take for your thesis. You should know how long you will be expected to wait after submitting. If you meet potential examiners, you should be able to tell them what deadline is expected of them if they agree to examine your thesis.

If you are studying abroad as an international student, you may need to apply for a bridging visa that will allow you to continue to live in your host country whilst your thesis is under review. You may have already secured a postdoctoral position or fellowship that requires your conferral of a doctoral degree prior to commencement. Being aware of how long you need to wait for the thesis revision is critical to being able to plan the next stage of your life and career.

Backing up your thesis

One of the most common issues I have seen among the doctoral students that I have consulted has been the **loss of data or writing time** due to digital failure, computer crashes, and document loss. You need to ensure from the beginning of your doctoral studies that you establish a reliable system for backing up your digital resources. Some of the main approaches I suggest are to back up to Dropbox (www.dropbox.com), Google Drive (www.google.com/drive/), or other cloud drives that you may have available for use.

I recommend that you keep a consistent approach to backing up your content throughout your candidature. Using more than one backup system each day/week is a very good way to ensure that you do not lose all the work that you are putting so much effort into.

I personally always keep the hard copies that I print at different stages of the revision process. I do this so I have a manual backup in case of complete digital failure. When establishing your backup system, you should confirm with your supervisor that the system you are employing is acceptable; particularly if you are pursuing work that poses a potential for developing intellectual property that requires certain checks and balances to be able to patent the concept.

Permissions

If you are publishing your thesis by including published articles in your chapters, you need to ensure that you secure permission to do so from the journals that now hold the copyright. It is easier to do this at the time of journal article publication, and it is something to ensure as you progress through your doctoral studies. Some journals will publicize their permissions policy on their website or in instructions to authors, indicating that they do or do not permit inclusion of their articles to doctoral theses.

> **YOU MUST OBTAIN PERMISSION TO INCLUDE PUBLISHED PAPERS TO YOUR THESIS**

Cotutelle or Joint Thesis

Some theses by publication may be submitted as a Cotutelle, or Joint Thesis, which is submitted to multiple institutions. If this is the case, you need to ensure that you follow the individual guidelines for each of these institutions for each thesis that you submit. You must note in each thesis that it is also being examined elsewhere; however, it will otherwise need to be written specifically for each institution. You may note this in the Statement of Originality in the preliminary pages, and some choose to also note this on the title page.

Sourcing information and preparing for all of these issues during the first stages of your PhD can be done "in between" all of your other tasks. Consider it a running "to do" list that you can work on without thinking too hard between experiments, or when you simply can't manage further deep thinking for the day.

END OF CHAPTER 2 SUMMARY
Practical Preparation

The basic planning steps for your thesis by publication have been discussed here. A range of key criteria must be defined in the preparation of your dissertation. The approaches covered include:

- You should consider the main sections that will constitute your dissertation.

- Various formatting issues must be considered when setting up your manuscript.

- Printing, binding, digital collections, examiners, timing, back-ups, and permissions should all be organized as you develop and deliver your thesis.

- Separate guidelines should be determined for each submission if you are pursuing a Cotutelle or Joint Thesis.

EXERCISE 2.1: CHECKLIST FOR THESIS LAYOUT

Create a checklist for the layout of your thesis. Refer to your institution's guidelines. What are the key sections that you will be including in your dissertation? Can you add to this checklist?

Prepages	
Title Page	
Statement of Originality	
Table of Contents	
List of Tables	
List of Figures	
List of Original Publications	
List of Contributors	
Acknowledgements	
Abstract/Summary	
Main body of work	
Introduction	
Literature Review	
Aims of Study	
Methods Chapter	
Research Paper Chapters	
Conclusions	
Summary	
Future Directions	
References/Bibliography	
Appendices	

EXERCISE 2.2: CHECKLIST FOR PRACTICAL CONCERNS

Create a checklist for the practical information that will support the development and delivery of your thesis. Some of the contents that you might include in your checklist are:

- Printing and binding requirements.
- Guidelines for examiner selection.
- Estimated time for examination.
- Approaches for backing up your content.
- What permissions are required for each article?

Chapter 2 – Downloadable Materials
Download from www.practicalacademic.com

- Exercise 2.1: "Checklist for thesis layout" – Word file containing a template.

CHAPTER 3

Preliminary Pages

In this chapter, we discuss the preliminary pages of the thesis and what type of content you include in them. As introduced in chapter 2, the preliminary pages outline the practical components of the thesis, providing support information regarding the work presented in the main body of the thesis. The preliminary pages (or "prepages") usually contain the following sections that frame the thesis prior to launching into the actual investigation presentation.

Page Numbers

A common practice for the prepages is to use Roman numeral lowercase page numbers (i.e. i, ii, iii, iv ...) — with the exception of the title page, which is not numbered. These are usually situated at the bottom of the page.

Title Page

The requirements for the title page of the thesis will vary between institutions, but generally it will include the following information.

- Title of the thesis in full.
- Names and degrees of the candidate.
- Name of the organization, institute, or group in which the research was carried out (if applicable).
- Name of the host university department.
- Date when thesis is/was submitted and/or re-submitted for the degree.
- Statement of presentation.

Most institutions will also request that you include their **logo** on the title page. A mock example of what you might include on your title page is shown below, in figure 3.1. Presentation format will potentially vary according to local guidelines.

Investigation of the Properties of Nautilus-derived Compounds and Secretions

Jerome Smith

Bachelor of Biotechnology (first class)
University of the Southwest

A thesis submitted in partial fulfilment of the requirements for the degree of
Doctor of Philosophy

Department of Chemistry,
Northwest University
Oceania

Submitted for examination: November 2012
Final Submission: August 2013

Figure 3.1: Mock title page of a thesis by publication.

The guidelines for title pages are usually identical for traditional theses and theses by publication. Some institutions will not provide clarity on title page requirements, and some may have department-specific guidelines.

Statement of Originality

A signed statement of originality or a declaration of originality is usually required to outline the following key points.

> 1: The work has not been submitted elsewhere for a higher degree.
>
> 2: The information sources in the dissertation are referenced/not plagiarized, and the work is original.
>
> 3: The appropriate ethics clearances were sourced; reference to these should be made.
>
> 4: The copyright holders have provided permission to reproduce the work in this thesis*.

*When you are producing a thesis by publication, the journals in which you published the work must provide their permission to include the paper in the thesis. Once you publish in a journal, you assign your copyright to that journal.

EXAMPLE: Brief statement of originality

This thesis is the result of my own work and includes nothing which is the outcome of work done in collaboration, except where specifically indicated in the text. This work has not been submitted for a higher degree to any other university or institution.

EXAMPLE: Longer statement of originality

I certify that the work in this thesis entitled "Investigation of the Properties of Myogenic Stem Cells and their Migration" has not previously been submitted for a degree, nor has it been submitted as part of requirements for a degree, to any university or institution other than Smithfield University. I also certify that the thesis is an original piece of research and it has been written by me. Any help and assistance that I have received in my research work and the preparation of the thesis itself have been appropriately acknowledged. In addition, I certify that all information sources and literature used are indicated in the thesis.

The research presented in this thesis was approved by the Smithfield University Human Research Ethics Committee, reference number:

    Human Ethics Approval   5301200486 — 2015

    Biosafety Approval   6121007875 — 2015

Some of the research presented in this thesis (chapter 4) was approved by the University of Jonestown Animal Ethics Committee. Confirmation of this approval was provided to the Smithfield University Animal Ethics Committee.

    Animal Ethics Approval: TAUTTQ/334/BiGENEIS — 2016

John Brand (4216 4688)
30 November 2016

> ***STATEMENT OF ORIGINALITY IN BRIEF***
> *Clarify work unpublished elsewhere.*
> *Clarify work is original and fully referenced.*
> *Provide evidence of ethics clearances.*
> *Confirm permission is given by copyright holders.*

Table of Contents

The table of contents is usually the last thing that you need to format prior to completing your final thesis draft. As you set out your document, you should leave a page with the heading "Table of Contents," which you can complete later. The table of contents is usually drafted from the headings that you marked up throughout the document as you wrote it.

The **document map/headings** provided in Microsoft Word are extremely useful in setting out your manuscript, and these are instrumental in creating your table of contents. You should familiarize yourself with the methods required to do this early in your doctoral studies. This will prevent you having to rush prior to submission.

> **TABLE OF CONTENTS IN BRIEF**
> *No page limit.*
> *Use Word headings.*
> *Last task before finalizing print copy.*

List of Tables and List of Figures

Including a list of tables and a list of figures in your thesis will aid your reviewers in being able to quickly access information, particularly if you have included summary figures that provide a quick visual guideline for the reader. I'm a big advocate of "a picture speaks a thousand words," and I find theses that employ visual/graphical support of concepts to be infinitely more accessible than those that fail to visually guide the reader through the content.

If you are using Microsoft Word to write your thesis, captions can be used to create a separate list of tables and/or figures. Tables and figures may be numbered sequentially throughout the manuscript; however, they are often numbered according to the chapter in which they appear (as is the case in this book). For example: Table 1.1, Table 1.2, 2.1, and so on; or Figure 1.1, Figure 1.2, Figure 2.1, etc.

EXAMPLE: List of tables/figures
An excerpt from a list of tables and another from a list of figures are both demonstrated here.

List of Tables
Table 1.1 Summary of water usage in Australia (2001–2011)......15
Table 1.2 Key regions submitting water data................................30
Table 1.3 Key contribution organizations..37
Table 2.1 Summary of methods in study..48
Table 3.1 Survey data 1..81
Table 3.2 Survey data 2..87

List of Figures
Figure 1.1 Model of regional area of investigation......................18
Figure 1.2 Rainfall map of Australasia..25
Figure 2.1 Data collection outline (flow chart)..............................47
Figure 3.1 Image of survey area..83

LIST OF TABLES/FIGURES IN BRIEF
Number sequentially through manuscript/chapter.
Use captions to create list in Word.
Aids reader in quickly assessing your work.

List of Original Publications
The list of original publications is good to include to demonstrate the overall content that you have delivered within the scope of your doctoral studies. Each of the articles should be assigned an **uppercase Roman numeral** that you will use to refer to that article throughout the thesis. An example of the content to include in the list of original publications is shown here.

EXAMPLE: List of original publications

This thesis is based on the following original publications, which are referred to in the text by uppercase Roman numerals. Original publications are reproduced with permission from their copyright holders.

I   Kuja-Panula J*, **Kitomäki M***, Yamashiro T, Rouhiainen A, Rauvala H (2003) AMIGO, a transmembrane protein in axon tract development, defines a novel protein family with leucine-rich repeats. *Journal of Cell Biology* 160(6): 963-973. doi: 10.1083/jcb.200309074a

II   **Kitomäki M**, Jones J, Smith MM, Rauvala H (2005) AMIGO in oncogenesis. *Nature Cell Biology* 290(8):34-42. doi: 19.1029/ncb.200508123a

III **Kitomäki M**, Smart J, Rouhiainen A, Rauvala H (2003) The role of AMIGO, in neural development in utero. *Submitted to Development.*

IV   **Kitomäki M**, Jones J, Smith MM, Rauvala H (2005) AMIGO in injury repair. *Cell, in press*

V   **Kitomäki M***, Jones J*, Smith MM, Rauvala H (2005) Binding characteristics of AMIGO: designing therapeutics for burn therapy. *Burns, accepted.*

* Equal contributors

You should include the doi (digital object identifier) numbers if the papers are already published, for ease of access to electronic versions of your manuscripts. Various **manuscript descriptors** may be included if the paper has not yet been published. These descriptors may include the following.

Accepted / accepted to [journal name] — where the manuscript has been reviewed and accepted for publication, but is not yet published.

Submitted / submitted to [journal name] — the manuscript has been submitted to a journal for review, and this journal name may be specified or not.

To be submitted to / to be submitted to [journal name] — the manuscript is intended for submission to a specific journal, but may not be ready yet.

In press — the manuscript is accepted and in the process of being published, but the article is not yet available and the journal is not specified.

In preparation — the manuscript is currently being prepared to be submitted.

You may have published articles during your doctoral studies that you do not wish to include in your main thesis. You can include them in this section to demonstrate your productivity. If they are relevant to the study but are not a key part of the work — for instance if they pre-date the main thesis work — you may include them to your appendices, at the discretion of your doctoral committee or supervisor.

EXAMPLE: Relevant publications

> Other publications not included to thesis are:
>
> **Kitomäki M**, Jules J, Smart M, Mouse M (2003) Novel techniques for delivery of mutagenic constructs. *Transgenic Techniques, 23(2):3-15.* doi: 15.1028/tt.20030813153a

Provided in Appendix:

Kitomäki M, Jules J, Mouse M (2002) Design of mutagenic constructs. *Transgenic Techniques, 22(1):28-34.* doi: 15.1028/tt.2002028345a

---

LIST OF ORIGINAL PUBLICATIONS IN BRIEF
Arranged in order of presentation in thesis.
Use Roman numerals to define publication number.
Must clarify publication status.

List of Contributors

Given that the thesis by publication includes research articles that are delivered by a team of researchers, it is important to clarify the role that you played in the completion of the work for each of the publications. It is critical that your examiners can gauge that you have made a substantial contribution to each of the journal articles being presented as part of your thesis by publication.

You should specify the contribution of others to the preparation of the thesis, or to individual parts of the thesis. Author contributions are specified here, as well as in acknowledgements and footnotes/endnotes. The thesis author would usually be the principal author of the manuscripts being presented, and evidence for this should be presented in the appropriate manner for the discipline. Examiners assess the quality and extent of the candidate's contribution.

Three main styles may be used here to specify the relative contributions made to joint author manuscripts.

1: YOUR CONTRIBUTION SPECIFIED

You may clarify your contribution to the work, omitting the other work performed by others, working on the assumption that anything that is not mentioned was not performed by you.

> I: In paper I, I performed the cloning experiments to create the DNA constructs required for the synthetic proteins and bioactivity assays. I performed all transfection and transformation experiments, and together with DJW did fermentation experiments, ion-exchange chromatography, and crystallization for pure protein extracts. The work was performed under the supervision of Prof. Robert Jones with the guidance of Dr Geoffrey Smith.

2: OTHERS' CONTRIBUTION SPECIFIED

You may choose to specify the work that others did in relation to the published manuscripts, working from the underlying assumption that you completed everything but that which is specified.

> I: In paper I, all experimental procedures and paper preparations were performed by myself, JER, with the exception of the following: (1) protein expression and crystallization was done together with DJW; (2) cell culture was assisted by TAM; and (3) paper revisions were made by all contributing authors, under the mentorship of RBJ and GNS.
>
> * Authors are referred to by their initials, full details in the original article.

3: ALL CONTRIBUTIONS SPECIFIED

A particularly elegant approach is to include details of all contributors to the manuscripts included in the thesis in a table, outlining the author's relative contributions. A mock example of the type of contribution table you might include in your thesis by publication is shown in figure 3.2. You might also provide a variation of this where you indicate percentage contributions by each author, or more specificity regarding their involvement in the work.

DIVISION OF LABOR IN CO-AUTHORED ARTICLES

AT — Alana Top; DC — Dale Cane; DD — Dephina Dean; LF — Lucy Frond; MR — Mike Riser; MW — Michele Wing; NL — Nancy Ligh

	I	II	III	IV	V
Conception and design	DD, MR, NL	MR, DD	NL, DD	DD, MR	DD, MR, MW
Planning and implementation	DD	DD, MR	NL, DD	DD, MR, MW	DD, MW
Data collection	DD, NL	DD	NL, DD	MW, DC, DD	DD
Analysis and interpretation	DD,	DD, MR, NL	DD, MW	DD, DC, MW	MW, DD
Writing the article	DD, AT, MR, NL, LF	DD, MR, AT	DD, MW, AT, MR	DD, AT, MW, MR	MW, DD, AT, MR
Overall responsibility	DD	DD	DD	DD	MW

Figure 3.2: Specifying each author's contributions in a table.

> **LIST OF CONTRIBUTORS IN BRIEF**
> *1–2 pages.*
> *Arranged relevant to articles.*
> *Must clarify your contribution to the work.*

Acknowledging Supervisors and Examiners

In the list of contributors, you may also include details of your supervisors and examiners, but this is relative to the advice provided by your institution. This is required to be included by some universities.

EXAMPLE: List of contributors — Supervisors/Examiners

Supervisor	Professor Jona Jonasson Department of Computing Smithfield University, Australia
Associate Supervisor	Associate Professor Richard Natale South Island Institute of Technology University of South Island, New Zealand
Internal Examiner	Professor Rob Jones Maths Hub Smithfield University, Australia
External Examiner	Doctor Tim Robbins Department of Engineering Espoo University, Finland

> **ACKNOWLEDGING SUPERVISOR IN BRIEF**
> *1–2 pages.*
> *Include affiliation and relationship to you.*
> *Follow university guidelines regarding their inclusion.*

Acknowledgements

Just about everyone that will pick up your thesis to read it, will read your acknowledgements. It gives the reader a chance to understand who you are as a person, and to develop some understanding of the support system around the work.

- People read your acknowledgements to get a feeling for who you are as a person. Do not overlook them.

- Use exceptional language.

- Try to group the acknowledgements into paragraphs.

In my experience, the acknowledgements are usually grouped into paragraphs and presented in the following order, and usually with a paragraph per grouping:

   1: Your source of scholarship and funding.
   2: Your supervisors and host institution/department.
   3: Your professional collaborators and colleagues.
   4: Your friends that kept you sane.
   5: Your family and/or partner.

EXAMPLE: Acknowledgements

> This investigation would not have been possible without the funding and support provided by the Infectious Diseases Council of Oceania, which provided my doctoral scholarship and grant

funding for the project. The Department of Biology at the University of Oceania provided outstanding facilities and an excellent scholarly environment within which to perform the work.

I am enormously grateful to my supervisors for supporting me through my doctoral studies. My principal supervisor, Prof Matti Jones always provided clear guidance and unwavering encouragement; my associate supervisor Liesel Smith shared her deep knowledge and investigative knowledge in medical engineering.

My colleagues in the Department of Biology and from the Institute of Infectious Diseases made the pursuit of this research an incredibly enjoyable endeavor. In particular I wish to thank: John Stone for his microscopy expertise; Lorraine Walton for her guidance in all thing PCR; Melanie Day for collaborating throughout these years; and Thea Rhodes for consistent encouragement and support. I am also immensely grateful to my colleagues in the HMRTV Research Centre, including: John for assisting with specimen collection; Anna for helping with formatting; Joseph for securing all my bookings; and Sanna for assistance with statistical analysis.

This marathon investigation would never have reached completion were it not for my wonderful friends that provided sanity breaks and moral support. Thank you so much for John, Anna, Joanna, Thom, Katherine, Tomiko, Xavier, Michael, and Dave.

Finally, my love and thanks to my family. Mum and Dad, you have never wavered in your support and belief in what I can do, thank you so much for everything. My partner in crime, Jonathan, and our little peanut Jo, you make everything worthwhile.

> **ACKNOWLEDGEMENTS IN BRIEF**
> *1–2 pages.*
> *Thanks to various supporters.*
> *Carefully presented (most read section of thesis).*

Abbreviations

You will no doubt utilize a range of abbreviations in the preparation of your thesis by publication. The preliminary pages should include a list of abbreviations that your readers can refer to as they come across acronyms and abbreviations that they are not familiar with. This list should be presented in alphabetical order, and focus on key words that you abbreviate throughout the thesis. The abbreviations list is typically one to two pages long and single spaced. Don't forget to provide the full terminology, and its abbreviation in parentheses, upon first use in the main body of your thesis.

EXAMPLE: Abbreviations list
Here is an excerpt from the abbreviations list that I included in my thesis (Rowland, 2003).

List of Abbreviations
Amino acids are abbreviated to three letter code.

ALS	acid labile subunit
CDE	chronic diabetogenic effects
CIS	cytokine-inducible SH2-containing protein
CYP	cytochrome P450
Da	daltons
dpc	days post coitus
DTT	dithriothreitol
ERK	extracellular signal regulated kinase
EPO	erythropoietin

G418   geneticin 418
GAS   gamma activated sequence
GH   growth hormone
GHBP   growth hormone binding protein
GHR   growth hormone receptor
GHIS   growth hormone insensitivity syndrome
GHRH   growth hormone releasing hormone
Grb2   growth factor receptor binding protein 2
Het   heterozygote
hr   hours
IGF-1 insulin-like growth factor I
IGFBP insulin-like growth factor binding protein
ILE   insulin-like effects
IRS   insulin receptor substrate
kDa   kilodaltons
KO   knock-out
KI   knock-in
lid   liver IGF-1 deficient
LIF   leukemia inhibitory factor

ABBREVIATIONS IN BRIEF
1–2 pages.
Arranged alphabetically.
Must be defined in full when first used in the text.

Abstract

The abstract should provide a synopsis of the overall findings of your thesis and is usually the last study-specific section that you write. It should encompass all of the papers presented, and any extra data provided to complement them. It is usually presented using between 200 and 400 words, or one to two pages. The specific word count is typically defined by the institution with which you are affiliated. The abstract should clearly summarize the main focus and outcomes of the doctoral work, and draw together the overall outcome of the thesis. You need to ensure that you clarify how the thesis has altogether addressed the gap in knowledge that you identified at the commencement of the study.

You can consider breaking the abstract up into paragraphs that represent different foci, as outlined in figure 3.3. This has been condensed to a one-page representation here, but it may be longer.

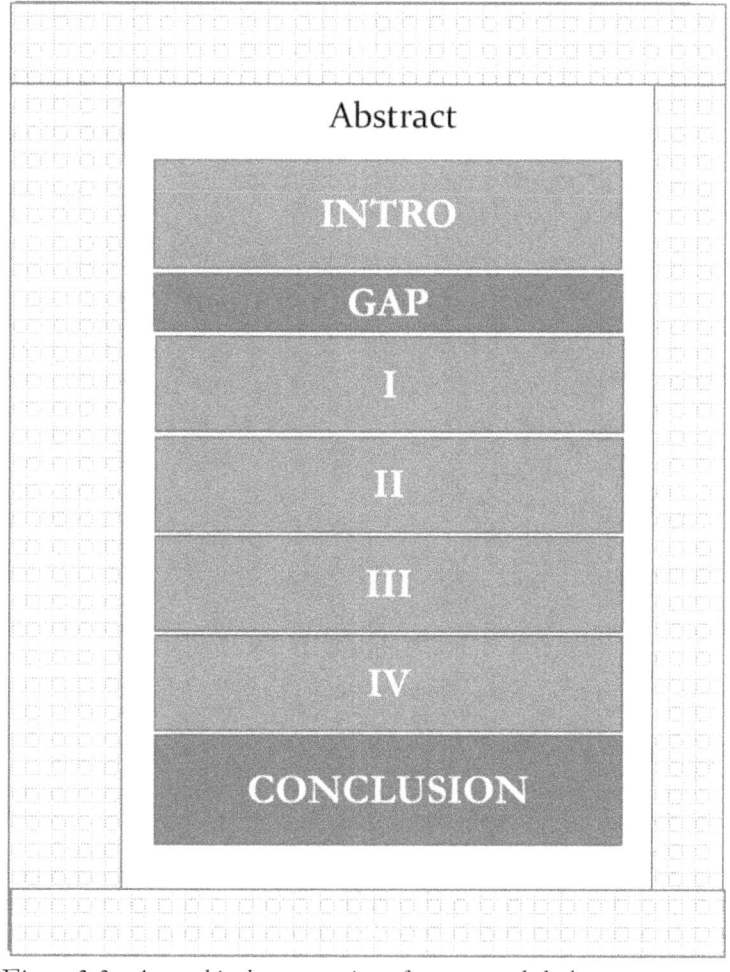

Figure 3.3: A graphical presentation of recommended abstract structure.

The introduction paragraph outlines the overall field that you are focusing on, leading to the gap in knowledge that you are specifically addressing in your thesis.

Reserve a paragraph for each of the papers you are presenting, written in order of how you present them in the thesis. Refer to them by their Roman numeral (I, II, III, etc.).

In the final paragraph, present the overall conclusions of the study and their relevance to the state of the art, that is, the latest advancements in the discipline. You may or may not mention how this work may be extended in future investigations.

> ***ABSTRACT IN BRIEF***
> *200–400 words / 1–2 pages.*
> *Summary of main findings.*
> *Presented in same order as chapters.*

END OF CHAPTER 3 SUMMARY
Preliminary Pages

This chapter has overviewed some basic considerations regarding the preliminary pages that you will include in your thesis by publication. This has covered the type of content you should include in key sections of the preliminary pages, and provide some examples of how you can deliver these sections. The main sections outlined in this chapter were:

- Title page.
- Statement of originality.
- Table of contents.
- List of tables and/or figures.
- List of original publications.
- List of contributors.
- Acknowledging supervisors/examiners.
- Acknowledgements.
- Abbreviations.
- Abstract.

EXERCISE 3.1: REQUIREMENTS FOR PRELIMINARY PAGES
Review the guidelines for thesis by publication at your institution and complete the following checklist regarding what you are expected to deliver for your preliminary pages. Consider any specific details that may be required by your institution.

CHECKLIST OF PRELIMINARY PAGES

Section	Include? (Details)
Title page	
Statement of originality	
Table of contents	
List of tables	
List of figures	
List of original publications	
List of contributors	
Acknowledging supervisors/examiners	
Acknowledgements	
Abbreviations	
Abstract	

EXERCISE 3.2: ACKNOWLEDGEMENTS

Who should you include in your acknowledgements in your thesis? Write your own list here so that you can keep track of those you wish to thank, so nobody is overlooked in your final submission. Consider the categories below and who/what should be included in each section.

Funding body:

Supervisor(s):

Department/University:

Colleagues:

Collaborators:

Friends:

Family:

Chapter 3 – Downloadable Materials
Download from www.practicalacademic.com

- Exercise 3.1: "Checklist of preliminary pages" – Word file containing a template.

CHAPTER 4

Introduction, Literature Review, and Aims

The main body of your thesis leading up to the presentation of your articles is the framework for your entire investigation. This section should bring the reader completely up to speed on the state of the art leading to the study that you completed. You need to ensure that you **clarify the gap in knowledge** that you are addressing in the context of your field and in general.

This section is often identical to the style that is required for a traditional thesis, so if you are unsure whether you will change to a traditional thesis closer to the end of your doctoral studies, this section can usually be adapted for both. Therefore, getting your introduction, literature review, and aims written early serves you well. You should revise the introduction regularly throughout your studies, in tandem with pursuing your physical investigations.

Completing a thorough literature review in your first year of your PhD will help you to get on top of the field, and enable you to troubleshoot issues that may arise during your experimental work with more clarity.

Introduction and Literature Review

You may include a brief (1–4 page) introduction to frame your overall literature review, or you may consider your literature review to be your introduction. This section typically spans anything from 5 to 50 pages in a standard thesis by publication; the length varies dramatically between individuals.

The literature review in the thesis by publication is essentially the same as in the traditional thesis. It presents an overview of the state of the art of the topic that is being presented in the thesis, to provide background sufficient for the reader to understand the reasoning behind the investigation(s). However, this differs from the individual introduction in the publications themselves, because it should more deeply explore the history of the discipline relative to all of the results presented in the entire body of work. The literature review should tie together the background as it is relevant to the entire thesis, leading toward the logical explanation of the aims of the investigation.

Variations on introduction in thesis by publication
Some theses by publication present variations on the traditional introduction. These might be as follows.

Reduced introduction size: because the introduction to each journal article that you are presenting can be substantial (depending on the target journal that you are publishing in). You may wish to reduce the size of your introduction for the overall dissertation. This can reduce repetition and make your thesis more succinct than a traditional thesis. Some universities may require no introduction at all for theses by publication.

Review article as introduction/literature review: some theses by publication include a literature review article as an introduction, which the student has published during their candidature and has listed in the list of original publications in the preliminary pages (chapter 2). This may be presented with extra introductory material to frame the article, as is standard for the results chapters (chapter 6).

PUBLISHING YOUR THESIS INTRODUCTION AS A REVIEW ARTICLE CAN BOOST YOUR PUBLICATION OUTPUT

Literature review presentation style

The introduction/literature review is usually **arranged in sections** that are presented systematically to provide an overview of the field leading to the study presented. The literature review should tie together all the topics presented in the thesis to frame a cohesive narrative. You may include tables or figures to demonstrate concepts.

> ***INTRODUCTION/LITERATURE REVIEW IN BRIEF***
> *More expansive than in a paper.*
> *History leading to current study.*
> *Overview of current state of the art.*
> *Relevance of current study.*
> *Naturally leads to aims of the work.*

Literature review tables and figures

Figures and tables may be included in this section, and are encouraged in order to demonstrate key concepts to the reader. These may take a variety of forms:

        1: Created by the author.
        2: Adapted from a published article.
        3: Taken from a published article.

If figures are adapted/taken from a published article, they should be fully referenced and the caption for the image or table should not be plagiarized. Permission should be obtained and noted if you use images from outside sources, see figure 7.1 caption as a style reference.

Some typical tables/figures that are often included in thesis literature reviews focus on the following:

Collation of data: You might include a graphic or table to summarize information or data that has been previously published. For instance, a molecular biologist might create a table of mutations previously studied; an economist might present a collation of information from multiple sources to demonstrate a trend or key concept, whilst a geologist might present a map outlining study areas and clarity on information relating to it.

Reference material: such as sequence maps of key DNA or proteins being investigated, added for reference. Details of regional study areas or trend data may also be included.

Overview of concept: a cartoon or flow chart might be included to demonstrate an overall concept of a natural event that you are studying (figure 4.3).

Key pictorial/image representation: some examples might include a rendering of a 3-dimensional protein structure with key residues highlighted, a cartoon of the intracellular mechanisms you are studying, or a pictographic of a volcanic process (figure 4.3).

Map/chart or reference image: a cartographic map, satellite image, overview of geographic sampling methods, microscopic image demonstrating cell types, or a surgical field.

<u>Summary table</u>
At the end of the introduction you will need to summarize the work being presented in the dissertation. You might choose to include a summary table to elegantly explain the overall content that you have discussed in your literature review. A summary table can clearly overview the main issue being addressed in the dissertation. For example, table 2 (figure 4.1 below) demonstrates the statistics of water resources in Australia. It clearly demonstrates the changes in different sources for water usage over a span of sixteen years, supporting the information covered in the literature review.

Table 2. Statistics of water resources in Australia (FRU, 2016)

					Annual Change Rate 1990-2016
Dammed water	Man made	na	na	2000 (42%)	na
	Naturally occurring	na	na	3200 (59%)	na
Reservoirs	Public	4200	3800	na	na
	Private	5000	5600	na	na
Usage rights (all)	Public	8000	7200	6000	15%
	Private	1000	3000	5000	500%
		800	14000	45000	500%
Home tank users					

Figure 4.1: Example of a summary table (mock).

Thesis summary figure

Using a pictorial image to outline the scope of the research study is one useful and interesting way to summarize topics that you have covered, as displayed in figure 4.2 and 4.3. Figure 4.3 elegantly expresses how the body of work fits within the major disciplinary foci that frame the research study. The reader can gain a clear understanding of the progression of the body of research from the first to last research paper presented as part of the thesis, and can quickly understand how the individual papers relate to each other.

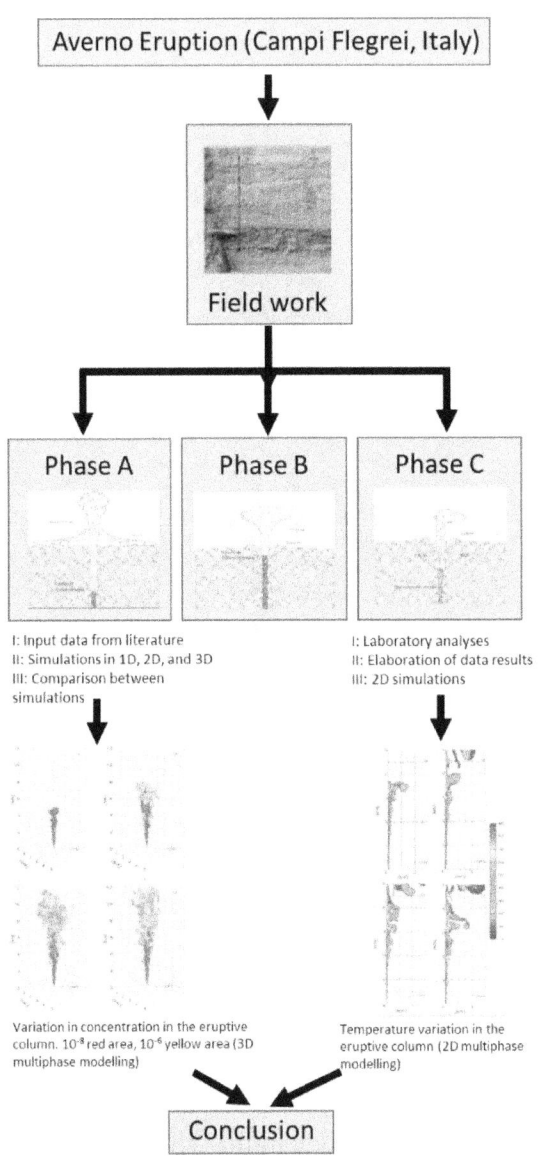

Figure 4.2: Example of a summary image. From Didonna (2009).

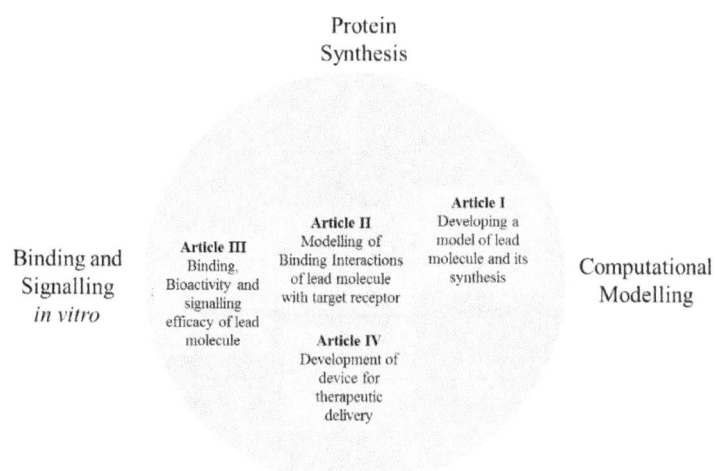

Figure 1. Position of individual articles I-V within different thematic areas.

Figure 4.3: Thesis summary figure.

Aims of Study

The aims of the study should be succinctly outlined following the introduction in typically one, sometimes two, page(s). The aims page is simple and straightforward to frame the next sections that are to be presented. Examples are shown below. The studies should be presented in the same order outlined in the list of publications, and referred to by their Roman numerals. If you have already presented an article as part of the introduction, this list of results/article chapters will commence at II. The goals of the studies should be listed in terms of what you wish to demonstrate in that chapter/article.

In the following examples, for simplicity, I will refer to a thesis study that presents four substantial papers for the dissertation.

EXAMPLE Aims page #1: Medical Genetics
Given the clear requirement to address the role of this protein in the development of carcinogenic states, the goal of this thesis investigation was to address the following key questions:

I. Where and during what stages of carcinogenesis does this protein become expressed and what are the dynamics of its activity?

II. When the protein is removed from carcinogenic cell lines, how does it impact the advancement of tumor growth?

III. How does knocking down the gene *in vivo* impact zebrafish and their response to carcinogens?

IV. What is the physiology of the XYZ knockdown mouse?

These studies are presented here in the following chapters.

EXAMPLE Aims page #2: Geology
Given the critical role that this sediment layer has proven to play in the evolution of the volcanic landscape, this investigation focuses on four major investigation topics.

I. Determining the presence of this sediment layer in the Indonesian volcanic field.

II. Analysis of the sediment in the Ecuadorian landscape.

III. Analysis of the sediment in the New Zealand volcanic chain.

IV. Relating the differences in these three main volcanic fields to each other in order to identify the role that this sediment plays in these fields and their geographical stability.

These studies are presented here in the following chapters.

EXAMPLE Aims page #3: Education

Digital approaches to delivering postgraduate training and support clearly require further improvements in the tertiary education space. Thus, this thesis focuses on the development and implementation of novel digital strategies to deliver this. This work is presented in the following chapters with these individual study foci:

I. Identification of key requirements for postgraduate training by surveying coordinators from 20 Australasian universities.

II. Collaboration with the department of computing to create a learning interface that addresses all of the key requirements outlined in study I.

III. Implementation of a test system in three test centers.

IV. Review and modification of the system, and wider distribution.

These individual investigations presented here will be referred to by their respective Roman numerals throughout this dissertation.

AIMS IN BRIEF
1–2 pages.
Outlines main goals of study relevant to articles presented.
Reference articles in Roman numerals.

END OF CHAPTER 4 SUMMARY
Introduction, Literature Review, and Aims

Here I have discussed some basic considerations regarding the introduction, literature review, and aims, which form integral components of both theses by publication and traditional theses. I considered how these sections could be presented and what might be included. The main considerations outlined here are:

- You must use this section to explain the logic underpinning the principal investigation that you are presenting for your thesis.

- Introduction/literature review figures and tables can summarize key concepts for the reader to easily understand.

- The introduction/literature review should lead to the rationale for the study being presented.

- A simple summary of the aims of the individual investigations should follow the introduction to frame the studies presented.

EXERCISE 4.1: KEY INTRODUCTION POINTS
Create a list of the key points that should be included in your introduction/literature review. Arrange them in a logical flow that naturally leads to your research question. Create a layout of thesis headings in your word processing program, which should be ready to go with correct settings as outlined in chapter 2.

References — chapter 4
Didonna, R. (2009). Dynamics of Averno2 eruption (Campi Flegrei, Italy) from stratigraphy to physical modeling. Thesis from University of Pisa (Italy). https://etd.adm.unipi.it/theses/available/etd-09232009-121525/

CHAPTER 5

A Word on Methods

Theses by publication may or may not include a separate methods chapter as part of the whole dissertation. You may choose to include a methods section in your thesis to provide **supplementary method information** to complement that which is delivered in the publications.

The method section might include more detail on specific approaches taken. Similarly, you might provide an **overview of the methods** used in the entire study, which can prove an easy reference resource for those assessing your dissertation. This provides clarity on the types of approaches taken throughout the study. The inclusion of a table of methods in this separate chapter can provide a reference point for the reviewer to identify the different methods that you have employed in your thesis papers. This approach can enable your reader to know where to look if seeking information about one specific approach that you have taken.

> **INCLUDING A METHOD SECTION CAN CLARIFY YOUR RESEARCH APPROACH**

The method section might take the form of a written narrative. For example:

> *The four articles in this thesis mainly employed quantitative analysis of gene expression and/or cell-analysis research methods (table 2). Article I employs ...*
>
> *Article II utilizes ...*

Or you may wish to present a method summary in a table, as shown in table 5.1.

Table 5.1. Methods and data employed in the articles.

Article	Analysis	Data
I	Part 1: Literature review. Part 2: Gap analysis of existing and required water sources in the entire Australian continent, with reference to current services and suppliers.	Part 1: peer-reviewed articles and gray literature on issues related to water resources and dependencies on different sources throughout Australia between 2001 and 2014 (n=46). Part 2: The Australian Water Board and services classification and record of national water supply provided by the Federal WB report released in 2015.
II	Regional mapping.	GIS data generated from Murray-Darling river basin. Sourced from state survey published in 2015.[a]
III	Qualitative review.	Perspectives of state water boards and commercial suppliers (n=50). Data collected through interview-delivered questionnaires during June–December 2015.
IV	Descriptive statistics and qualitative content analysis.	Perspectives of local households gathered through open- and close-ended surveys (n=100). Data collected through interview-delivered questionnaires during December 2015 in the Murray-Darling river basin.

Some very savvy theses include flow charts or graphs outlining the advancement of the research approaches taken through the course of the papers presented. Classical foci that might employ a flow chart include: sampling methods, cloning, injection, selection, cell biology, animal breeding strategies, tests, and human studies. Clinical theses may include a flow chart outlining the selection of patients included in the investigation (figure 5.1).

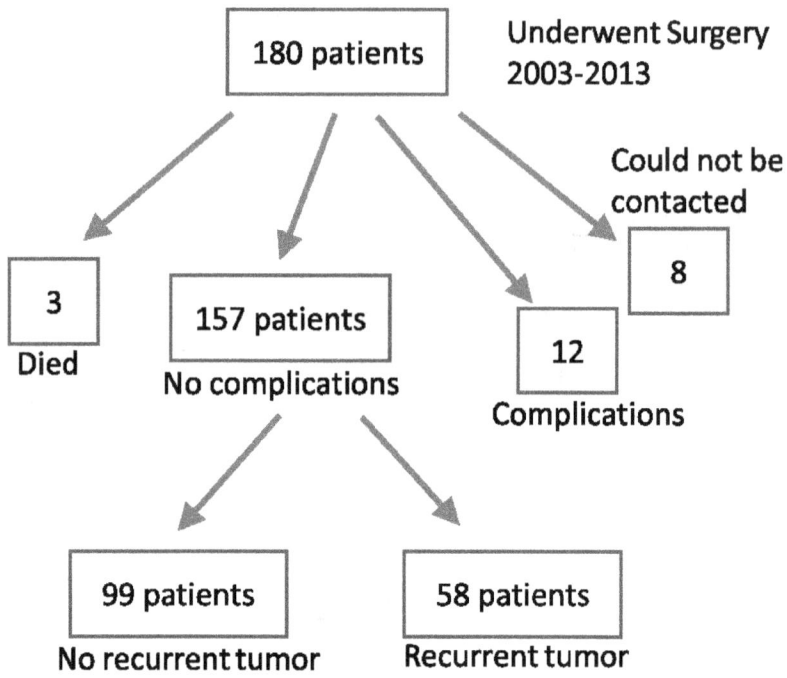

Figure 5.1: Flow chart for patient selection to a study.

Those pursuing resource-heavy investigations may wish to include a summary of the resources that were employed in their investigations.

Some key methods may be depicted in this section to clarify how they were pursued in the studies described in the results/paper chapters. For instance, a detailed cloning strategy might be outlined in graphical detail in this chapter (figure 5.2).

GRAPHICAL PRESENTATIONS OF YOUR METHODS ARE USEFUL FOR OTHER PRESENTATION FORMATS

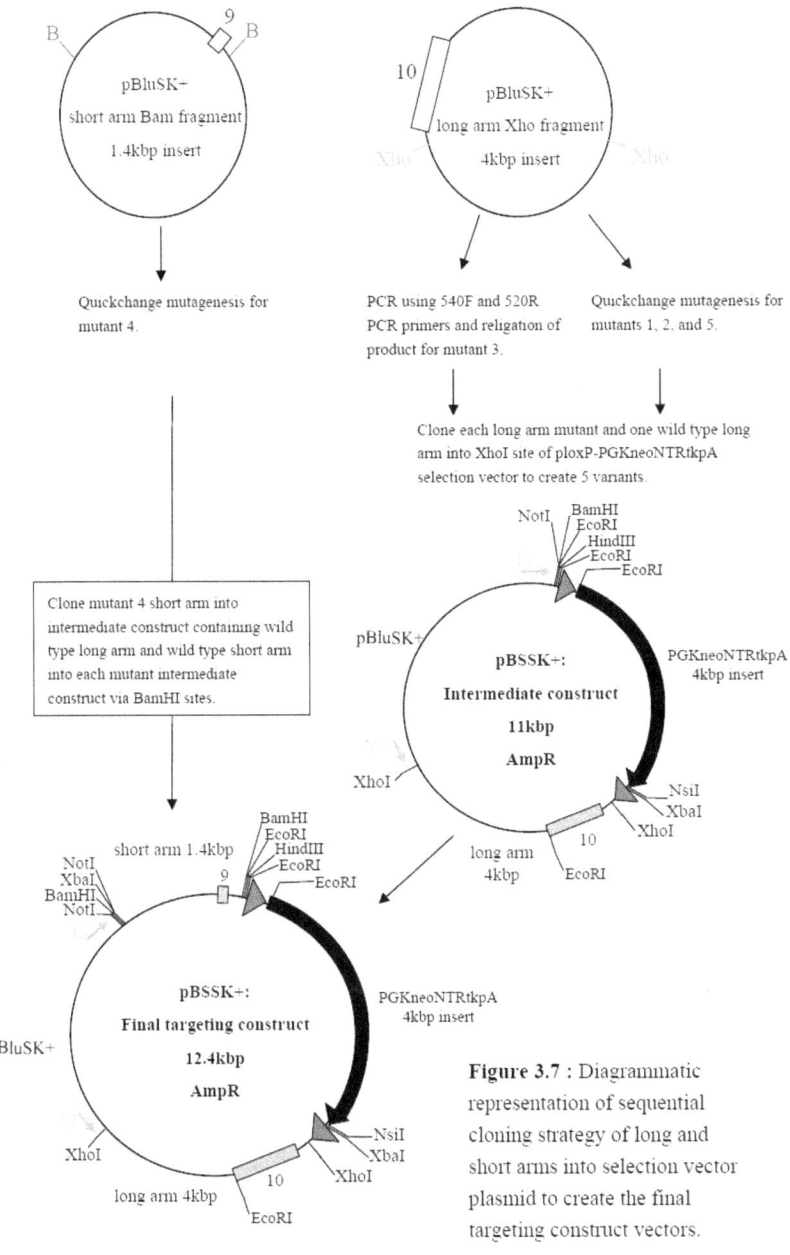

Figure 5.2: Outline of construct cloning strategy (Rowland, 2003).

Differences From Traditional Theses

The methods that you might include in a thesis by publication will differ in a few ways from those that you present in a traditional thesis. Your method section will be more complementary to those presented in the publications, aiming to provide the reader with further information that they may otherwise have to source for themselves elsewhere. For instance, it is standard in journal articles that methods are referenced from earlier published articles rather than described in full. Any specific changes made to the referenced methods may be noted. It may help your reader to better understand your work if you incorporate a more detailed method to complement the study you include in your thesis. Similarly, it provides you with the opportunity to frame how your methods in your different chapters link together. This is usually implicit in traditional theses, where a central method section is standard practice.

Methods Paper Chapter

Depending on your discipline, you may find the opportunity to present your methodology as a research article in its own right, and this should not be overlooked as an approach to boost your publication output during your doctoral studies. If you manage to publish a methodology paper for an approach that proves to be related to or critical for the rest of the body of work that you are presenting, you should certainly include it as a part of your thesis by publication. Whether you include this as a "results" chapter or frame it as a "method" chapter is entirely up to the discretion of you and your doctoral advisors, but this can significantly strengthen your dissertation and the following work stemming from the methodology.

> **PUBLISHING A METHOD PAPER CAN BOOST YOUR RESEARCH OUTPUT**

END OF CHAPTER 5 SUMMARY
A Word on Methods

Here I have discussed some basic considerations regarding a potential methods section that you may choose to include in your thesis by publication. The main topics addressed here are:

- Various content may be included in a thesis by publication methods chapter.

- How a thesis by publication methods section differs to that of a traditional thesis.

- You might include a published method in this section as part of your thesis by publication.

- A range of examples of tables and figures that you might include are presented.

EXERCISE 5.1: METHOD SUMMARY
Write a summary of all methods that you employ in your doctoral studies. Identify any that, for clarity, could be:
- graphically summarized,
- tabulated, or
- presented as a method paper.

References — chapter 5
Rowland, J.E. (2003) Trangenic analysis of Growth Hormone Receptor intracellular signaling pathways. *University of Queensland doctoral dissertation.*

CHAPTER 6

Results/Papers Chapters

The main difference in preparing a thesis by publication versus a traditional thesis is the inclusion of research papers instead of results chapters. For most institutions, students may include published papers presented **in the format of the original published article**, without making changes to match the style presented in the remainder of the thesis. Each article is standalone and delivers a research study that is **fully self-contained**, and each may be referred to by its Roman numeral, which you assigned in the preliminary pages. However, some considerations should be made in the presentation of these publication chapters.

Advance Planning

In order to promote the most efficient use of time and effort during your doctoral studies, it is absolutely essential that you **strategically plan the publications that you wish to include in your thesis** (table 6.1). As such, as you are reading through this chapter and this whole book, you need to take on board the ideas presented to ensure that you have a clear idea of how you are going to publish and/or present your work in a way that will add value to your primary goal of a thesis by publication.

If you present key information as a conference proceeding (for instance), you need check whether you will be able to include that proceeding in your thesis. Familiarizing yourself with your university guidelines, and asking questions to understand the framework in which you are delivering your work as you launch into your doctoral studies, is critical to making informed and clear decisions about the thesis that you will present.

Table 6.1: Chapter planning.

Chapter	Article focus	Type of publication
3, Paper I	Cloning and *in vitro* study.	Conference proceeding.
4, Paper II	Zebrafish investigation.	Journal article.
5, Paper III	Mouse analysis.	Journal article.
6, Paper IV	Human studies.	Journal article (in press).

Publication Status

Institutional guidelines should specify what types of publications you can include in your thesis. This issue has been touched upon briefly in chapter 2 (list of original publications) regarding how you should communicate the types of articles you are presenting, but here I describe further what these categories include.

Published journal article: Published journal articles are the standard content to be included in research theses by publication. Articles of the highest possible quality/ranking are preferred. This may be due to their acknowledged reverence within your discipline. Alternatively, higher impact factor articles are preferred in some disciplines. The complete details of the publication — including a doi link — should be included. Permission to include the article should be made clear in the statement of originality at the start of the thesis, and the article should be included in its original format.

Article accepted for publication: If the article has been accepted for publication, the complete details of the publication — including a doi link (if available) — should be included. Permission to include the article should be made clear in the statement of originality at the start of the thesis, and the article should be included in its original format.

Submitted journal article: If the article has been submitted for publication to a journal, or as a conference proceeding, this should be clarified in the list of publications (preliminary pages) and in the chapter where the paper is being presented. The article may be presented in the submission format that is accepted for the target journal. It may alternatively be presented in the format of the main body of the thesis (introduction, discussion, etc.), although references remain central to the article. The article should be noted as "*submitted*" or "*under review.*"

Prepared journal article: Your article may be prepared but not yet submitted when you finalize your thesis. Whether you may include this in your thesis by publication is at the discretion of your institution. However, it should be noted in the list of publications as "*prepared*" or "*not yet submitted.*"

You may wish to note where you intend to submit the manuscript: e.g. "*to be submitted to Nature.*" This can happen often when your article may have been rejected from its first target journal, or if you hope to add more data prior to submitting to a journal but after the completion of the thesis. The format should follow the main body of the thesis, or the format of your target journal, and referencing remain central to the article.

Published conference proceeding: Some conferences (often discipline specific) request the submission of substantial conference proceedings, which constitute a large amount of data that is comparable to a journal publication. These are usually substantial enough to warrant inclusion as a thesis chapter. They may be referred to in the same manner as outlined for regular journal articles that are included in the thesis.

> **PUBLICATION STATUS SHOULD BE CLARIFIED IN THE LIST OF PUBLICATIONS & IN THE CHAPTER WHERE IT IS PRESENTED**

Mixed or Combined Results/Publication Chapters Approach
Some institutions accept study results presented as traditional chapters as well as published or prepared journal articles. In this case, the same rules apply regarding the inclusion of the publication chapters, and the traditional results sections should follow the formatting and layout of the rest of the thesis. Nonetheless, as for the published articles, the references may continue to be listed specifically for that chapter, and not necessarily centralized to the main references chapter/bibliography listed at the end of the thesis.

Foreign Language Articles
If you wish to include articles that have been published in a language other than that in which you are submitting your thesis, you will likely be requested to present an official or certified translation. In some circumstances, English language journals allow resubmission of data presented in non-English language journals as a new article. If you are presenting an article that fits into this category, you should ensure that you confirm the requirements of your institution well in advance to allow for time for any translations or permissions that may be required. Clarity and detail in this instance is essential.

Publishing Platforms
Various disciplines follow individual guidelines regarding publication and publication types. Different platforms will be standard for different research disciplines. A range of various platforms are discussed here.

Traditional journal article

Traditional journal articles are generally accepted for inclusion in theses by publication. These constitute journals that accept submissions of original research papers, which undergo peer review to decide whether the manuscript is a worthy contribution to the research field that the journal focuses on. Traditional journal articles may include supplementary data which supports the main body of work that is being presented. Typically, **supplementary data should be included in the results chapter** presenting the journal article, rather than in an appendix.

Digital Platforms

Arxiv platform (https://arxiv.org/) is a platform run by the Cornell University Library for the publication of preprint articles in a range of disciplines. The disciplines include mathematics, physics, astronomy, computer science, quantitative biology, statistics, and quantitative finance. Not all of the articles presented to the archive reach publication in a journal, and some are submitted to a journal in tandem. Although the article is not peer reviewed, moderators do gauge the relevance of the articles submitted.

Further Arxiv platforms are being released to focus on other discipline foci, including Biorxiv (http://biorxiv.org/) for biology — run by Cold Spring Harbour — and SocArxiv (currently under development) for social sciences. Beyond Arxiv, you may also consider using Figshare (www.figshare.com) or the Social Science Research Network (SSRN: www.ssrn.com).

Conference proceeding

As discussed above, some disciplines place emphasis on the presentation of substantial conference article submissions. This can constitute the presentation of a paper that is specifically for the conference, and which will be peer reviewed and included in published conference proceedings. Conversely, many conferences may simply involve the presentation of an abstract. Whether you may include a conference proceeding in your thesis by publication is at the discretion of your advisor, supervisor, and university.

Open Access, or Not?

Journals generally approach the publication of your work in one of two ways. The first is that they publish your material and retain the copyright over the work, charging readers to have access to the journal.

Alternatively and more recently, journals have adopted an increasingly widespread option for authors to pay for open access of their articles, suggesting that authors pay for the privilege of others reading their work. Some journals also operate in an entirely open-access style, providing free access to readers at no extra cost to the reader or author.

If you are seeking to understand the publishing practice of any specific journal, you might consider consulting the free service hosted by Nottingham University: SHERPA RoMEO. This can be accessed at http://www.sherpa.ac.uk/romeo/index.php. Here you can gain some ideas about the rules and regulations that any journal might have. The site states: "RoMEO is a searchable database of publisher's policies regarding the self-archiving of journal articles on the web and in Open Access repositories."

As a doctoral student, it is worth making time to meet with your **university research librarians** to discuss your publication strategy. You can gain some excellent insight into not only what approaches you can take in publishing your work, but also on databases and resources that can improve and inform your critical review of the literature as you prepare your thesis.

Predatory publishers

When you are considering publishing your work, it is important to be aware of predatory publishers, which have become a concern for academics in recent times. There is an increasing incidence of questionable, unethical, and often exploitative behaviors seen in some new publishing organizations. This is a significant issue, especially given the assignment of the copyright of your materials once you agree to publish them. Predatory publishers may practice a range of problematic approaches, which are described here.

> **Spamming:** unsolicited requests and invitations to use your material in a book, or to submit your research to a journal, which the publishers can arrange on your behalf.
>
> **Little or no peer review**: many predatory open-access publishers accept articles quickly, and with little quality control in the form of peer review. In this way, fake manuscripts can reach publication quite easily. If you choose to publish your quality work in this type of journal, you are underselling the value of your research.
>
> **Poor clarity in the publication process**: descriptions of fees for publishing an article in an open-access journal may not be made clear until after the article is accepted and ready to be published, thus blindsiding the author(s) who must then pay unexpected fees.
>
> **Fakery**: The journal may use a fake address or fake editors, or indicate that certain people are connected to the journal without their knowledge. Fake impact factors, or absence of impact factors, may be evident. Similarly, the journal may model itself on more established and highly regarded journals, thereby making their product appear to be above board and of high value.

Predatory publishers undermine the legitimacy of the practice of publishing in scientific journals. A "white list" of above-board journals is operated by the Directory of Open Access Journals (https://doaj.org).

Predatory publishers also target **theses published by recent graduates**. They approach the graduate with email and phone inquiries to request that they publish their thesis as a digital book that they can market via online booksellers, paying a small percentage of any profit to the student that provided the material.

> **CASE STUDY: Predatory publishers**
>
> A new PhD student had just completed her one-year postgraduate research project, including a short thesis describing the work that she had performed. In the first few months of her subsequent PhD studies, she was approached by a publishing company. They inquired whether she would be interested in publishing her thesis as a book with them. Upon performing an internet search for the company name coupled with "predatory publisher," many results came back indicating the publishing company would actually publish the thesis online, and would skim all but a small percentage of the profit (which they would feed back to the author), and that they would claim the copyright over the content in the process.

Formatting

I have consulted many students that have completely reformatted the research papers they intend to include in their thesis by publication so that they match the style of the entire thesis. Reformatting published journal articles to match the formatting style of the thesis can be time consuming, but it is usually unnecessary. **No reformatting of the publications is required by most institutions.** Be sure to inquire about this early, not only with the university/institution with which you are studying but also with the necessary journals. Do the latter when you seek permission to reproduce the manuscript in your thesis. Journals may not wish for you to reproduce the content in a format different to that which they have published.

Assuming that you may reproduce the articles in their original format, be sure to establish how you will embed them into your manuscript for printing. I have seen two approaches.

1. Insert the article after a certain page, where the article carries no page numbers intrinsic to the thesis. In this case the article is list in the table of contents as appearing after a given page number.

2. Embed the journal manuscript to include page numbers within the dissertation. In this case you can assign each page of the journal article a page number in your thesis.

The latter approach is more elegant; however, both are usually acceptable practice. Be certain to determine how you will embed your articles well before the end of your candidature, allowing yourself time. Seek help from professional or experienced design/formatting people where necessary.

Arranging the Publication Chapters
The publication chapters should be presented in order of their relevance to the flow of the study, which may not be chronological. It is important to create a flow of information that fits with the overall story presented in a body of work. Publications may be under review for varying lengths of time after submission to a journal. As such, even if you submit an article that launches your thesis first, it can well end up being the second or third to be published (see Chapter 1, Target Journals). Thus, the publication date does little to represent the article's standing in the order of presentation of the work.

Introducing the Article
To better introduce the publication within the scope of the overall study, a one- to two-page introductory section can be included in the publication chapters. This short introduction helps the reader to orientate the relevance of each publication in the framework of the entire investigation.

How can you commence your introduction pages?

Article I
This paper is based on an analysis of ...
OR
Given the need to address this key issue, this article presents an investigation into...

Article II
Based on the outcomes of Article I, the next natural step to drive the work forward was to address ...
OR
Now that the role that this molecule plays in in vitro cell models of cancer has been defined (I), attention will now be focused to...

Summarizing the Article

Once the paper is presented, you may also include a summary section that ties up the relevance of the data presented in the context of the overall study. You may allude to the next logical step in the overall thesis study, thus setting the scene for the introduction of the next publication chapter.

How can you commence your summary pages?

Article I
Here we have demonstrated that X functions in a key role related to ...
OR
In order to further explore this concept, a more relevant model should be developed, and this will be pursued in the next chapter.

Article II
Here we have expanded on the outcomes of Article I to further prove the role of X in a more appropriate model. Next, the focus of this thesis will be on investigating its role in clinical conditions.

Permissions

If you are including published journal articles, you need to ensure that you have **permission from the copyright holders** to include the articles in your thesis. Once you agree to allow a journal to publish your work, they usually hold the copyright of that content. In fact, they may provide stipulations on how you may reproduce the article in your thesis, and you are required to follow these. This should be resolved around the time of publication rather than assuming it is fine and then rushing to accommodate as you prepare to submit your dissertation.

If a journal denies you permission to include the article in your thesis, which does occasionally occur, you may include the web link for the reviewers to access the material. That said, it is rare to encounter a journal that will not allow you to include an article in your thesis. How productive would your research sector be without PhD students? **PhD students are the driving force behind academic innovation.**

Repetition

Some PhD students express concern about the fact that they may be repeating information in the introductions presented for each paper, as well as the main thesis introduction. Whilst you will need to cover certain background for each article, the introduction for a research paper should be tailored to the material being presented in that article. In comparison, the main introduction should be a complete overview of the field leading to the overall dissertation. Remember that you are not permitted to simply copy sections of your articles, thus plagiarize your own articles, as you prepare your literature review. Each article and the central literature review should be independently written. Try summarizing, paraphrasing, and quoting where required.

Earlier Studies/Partial-Candidature Papers

Sometimes **earlier studies** that you completed prior to commencing your doctorate studies will result in papers that you publish during the time you are enrolled as a PhD student. If you wish to include this type of paper as a result chapter in the thesis by publication because it completes the study overall, it is critical to clarify if the work has been presented for a dissertation previously, and to clarify exactly which aspects of the work were carried out as part of the PhD. This is noted in the contributor's and list of publications in the preliminary pages, as well as in the results chapter itself. Nonetheless, this type of lead-up investigation is usually included to an appendix as reference material (table 6.2).

Pre-Candidature Papers

If you published work prior to the commencement of your doctoral studies that underpinned the work you carry on to present in your thesis, you may consider including that article as an appendix to the thesis, as a reference for your reader. This may include work completed for your master's studies, or as an employed/volunteer researcher prior to commencing your postgraduate candidature. This work will generally not be accepted to form a chapter in your dissertation. An exception is where the work was partially completed prior to your enrollment as a PhD student, and then fully completed during your enrollment (see above, *vide infra*). In such cases, you must clarify this in your contributions list in the preliminary pages (chapter 3), and preferably also in the chapter itself (table 6.2).

Multiple Doctoral Authors

Sometimes doctoral students may collaborate on their research, resulting in joint authorships on one paper. In this case, both students may usually be permitted to include the paper in their thesis by publication, but their individual contributions must absolutely be clarified (see "List of Original Publications" in chapter 2). This information should also be clarified in the results chapter itself, perhaps as a footnote or highlighted point of clarification. If doctoral students collaborate on several studies, they will typically alternate first authorships.

EXAMPLE — multiple doctoral authors
This article is also submitted to Homerville University as part of the dissertation of Anna J. Smith, who collaborated on the project. Our individual contributions are outlined on page 15 in the List of Contributors.

Table 6.2: Common issues in presenting publication chapters

Concern	Issue	Resolution
Permissions	Copyright held by journal.	Obtain permission from copyright holder.
Repetition	Individual introductions may repeat content.	Tailor introductions to specific content focus.
Partial-candidature Papers	Some work completed prior to candidature.	Clarify specific doctoral work in prepages and chapter.
Pre-candidature Papers	Relevant work completed/published prior to candidature.	Include article to appendix and clarify relevance in prepages and introduction.
Multiple Doctoral Authors	One research paper used in two different student dissertations.	Clarify individual contributions in prepages and result chapter.

Location of Publication Chapters

In this book, we assume that the results chapters that are presented as published articles are embedded to the thesis in the following order:

- Preliminary Pages
- Introduction/Literature Review
- Aims
- Methods
- Results I – Paper I
- Results II – Paper II
- Results III – Paper III

- Results IV – Paper IV
- Discussion/Conclusions
- References/Bibliography
- Appendices

However, some may present their thesis in a way that they summarize the study in a cohesive narrative, referring to the journal articles throughout, and then amending them to the back of the thesis as reference material. The structure may then look like this:

- Preliminary Pages
- Introduction/Literature Review
- Aims
- Methods
- Results Overview
- Discussion/Conclusions
- References/Bibliography
- Appendix I – Paper I
- Appendix II – Paper II
- Appendix III – Paper III
- Appendix IV – Paper IV

If you follow the latter style in your thesis, you may choose to include an abridged results section, where you present the main findings for the reader, referring to the paper appendices where necessary. The paper appendices usually lack introductory and summary pages when presenting in this style.

END OF CHAPTER 6 SUMMARY
Results/Papers Chapters

Here I have discussed concerns relating to the publication chapters for a thesis by publication. Some of the issues covered regarding the presentation of your publication chapters, include:

- What types of articles can be included in the dissertation.

- The arrangement of the publications should present the overall study as a holistic narrative.

- Permissions are required before publishing the papers in your dissertation and formatting requirements should be determined.

- Take time to consider where you will publish and how it will impact the quality of your thesis.

- Use short introductions and summaries around the paper to help frame your investigation and promote flow between concepts.

- Clarify your contribution to each article.

- Previously published articles may be included in the appendices, or in a chapter if a substantial proportion of the work was performed during candidature.

- Alternative styles may be employed when you are presenting your results in a thesis by publication, including the amendment of the articles to an appendix at the end of the dissertation.

EXERCISE 6.1: FLOW CHART OF YOUR PAPERS
Create a flow chart highlighting the linkage between concepts presented in each of the research articles/studies. Note how you might link the chapters together to form a cohesive narrative. What specific points will you include in each of the introductory and summary sections flanking your publications?

References — chapter 6
Marina Pantcheva (2017)
http://site.uit.no/english/writing-style/citationstyles/
Accessed on 6th April 2017.

CHAPTER 7

Discussion, References, and Appendices

The discussion, references, and appendices tie together the entire thesis after presenting the study chapters. How you may address them in the context of your thesis by publication is discussed in this chapter.

Discussion

The discussion is a critical component of your dissertation, that draws together your findings and critically appraises the relevance and scope of your work in the context of the discipline as a whole. The **discussion** should present all the study findings and relate their outcomes to the state of the art covered in the introduction. It should clarify how this new work has contributed to the field. This section usually provides an overview of the study chapters in order of their inclusion, and then presents the narrative of the entire thesis study and how it contributes to the field overall. You may continue to **refer to the studies by their Roman numerals** for clarity throughout this section. Once you have discussed the overall contribution of the work, the conclusions should outline the main findings in brief.

Throughout this whole section, you should consider the limitations of the work and how they may be resolved in future investigations. You should introduce the future directions that you will potentially pursue to address these concerns and take the study further. You may choose to include figures or diagrams in this section to clarify the outcomes of your research. These often include summaries of the data that you presented in multiple chapters to form a cohesive narrative. You might also present a model of your findings that you have created in response to the data you have obtained, postulating a new conceptual model.

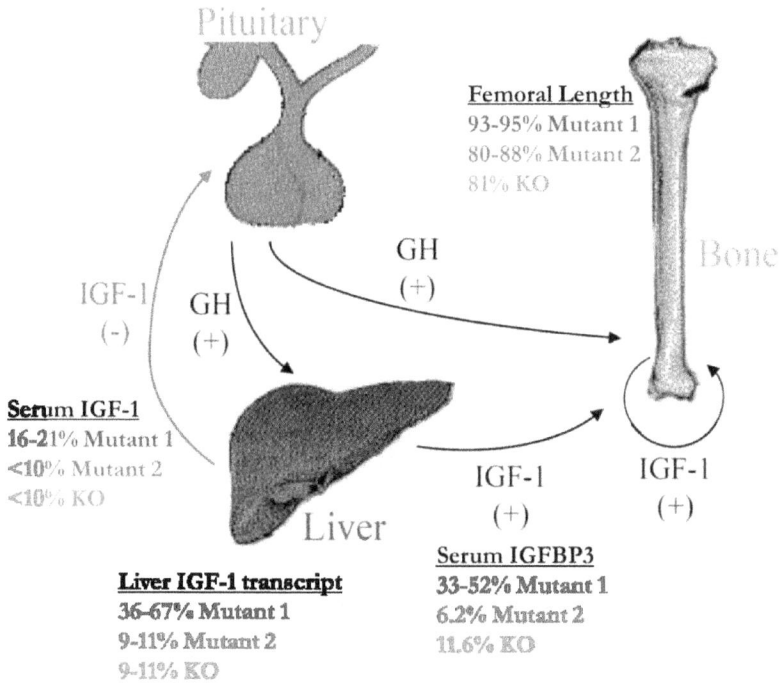

Figure 7.1: Example of figure summarizing major findings for the discussion section which represents the model derived from several results chapters. Adapted with permission from Rowland (2003).

Note keeping throughout candidature

You should continually make notes about ideas for things that you can include in your discussion. You should take notes throughout your doctoral training, but particularly after you begin your data collection. Your ideas about the meaning of your research outcomes will incubate over time, and the act of daily reflection (or at least regular ongoing reflection) will help you to deepen your perspective. This should be tied in with ongoing expansion of your reading of the literature, which will also broaden your view in tandem, potentially providing you with alternative perspectives on your research findings. As you follow this approach, I recommend keeping a notebook or journal nearby, where you can record ideas that you have about your work. You might employ this for various ideas.

Types of notes that you might take

- Figures you might develop to include in the thesis.
- What your latest results mean in the grand scheme of things.
- Potential experimental approaches you can take next.
- How to troubleshoot issues you are confronting or have confronted (this might be included in the discussion as a potential future direction if you lack the time to address the issue during your candidature).
- Potential collaborators or service providers that could help to advance the work.
- Interesting observations that you notice (this should also be noted in the laboratory book where possible).
- Notes on the next research articles that you might read.

Students who pursue more technical experimental research may not appreciate the **intensely creative** aspect of pursuing academic research, which becomes increasingly important as you progress through your research doctorate and on to a research career.

Ideas will come to you when you least expect it, so keeping some form of note taking device or notebook with you — at all times — can serve you well for when ideas hit you. Throughout your studies, this approach will strengthen the overall discussion that you ultimately sit down to write once you have completed your research papers. Regularly transferring these ideas to digital bullet pointed or short section notes will also minimize the time that you need later to put all of the information together in a cohesive narrative.

> **REGULAR REFLECTIVE PRACTICE IS KEY TO A STRONG DISCUSSION**

<u>Drafting the discussion</u>
How you put your discussion together can dictate how your reviewer will perceive your overall ability to interpret the relevance and contribution of your body of work to the field. It is well worth creating a well-structured and clear summary of your research, relating it to your discipline and how it contributes to the state of the art.

The sections should naturally flow into each other, and may present overriding themes that don't necessarily follow the order of presentation of the results chapters.

<u>EXAMPLE: summarizing the findings from the chapters</u>
In this study, new key factors involved in the process of cell recruitment during injury repair have been characterized. Four different transcription factors were identified and characterized as novel proteins localized to the cells infiltrating the injury space (I). When these factors, Tho1, Fry2, Ser4, and Pol1, were deleted in cells, cell migration was impaired (II). Injury repair was poor when these factors were deleted in both zebrafish (III) and mouse models (IV, V).

A classical approach would be to introduce the individual study outcomes again, explaining how they flow into each other and remembering to refer to them with their Roman numerals. This can be strengthened by a graphical representation of the overall study. Once you have laid this framework, you can then explore significant themes of the body of work relating to key focal points in your discipline. You might explore potential areas that require further investigation, or point out weaknesses in your work or the work of others. You may discuss a major focal point that runs throughout your investigation.

> EXAMPLE: significant themes
>
> The transcription factor Thol has been identified in several studies as upregulated during organ generation and tissue development (42, 57, 89). This investigation is the first to describe the role of Thol in injury repair. The nuclear localization of this factor during cell migration (I, II) and cell recruitment to replenish tissue (III, IV) is the first description of this role. This factor has previously been described to translocate to the nuclear compartment when cells are stimulated by CSF1, which is naturally upregulated during injury repair as a chemoattractant (52, 90).

The Discussion as a Review Paper

Another way to boost your publication output from your doctoral studies is to publish our discussion as a review paper. In the past, this has often come about from completed theses. Indeed, even if you choose to write a classical discussion within your dissertation, I encourage you to write a review of your topic as soon as you submit your doctoral thesis. If you have time to write and submit your discussion as a published review, there is no reason that you cannot submit this paper as a component of your thesis by publication.

Referencing

Referencing the work of other authors acknowledges their contribution to the research, and must be properly included in standardized format. The references listed at the end of the thesis need only to cover the components of the thesis that surround the publications you are presenting. That is, the references intrinsic to the publications should be presented in the result/paper chapter, but they do not also need to be included in the "References/Bibliography" chapter of the thesis. This makes sense, because you will be presenting different articles that will use a variety of formats and styles. Two referencing styles are most common in academic theses: Vancouver style and Harvard style (Pantcheva, 2017).

<u>Vancouver style referencing</u> is common for health and physical sciences, and involves the assignment of an Arabic number for each reference in order of its use. The style in which you list the reference numbers can vary.

You can list the number in round brackets (1), square brackets [2], superscript[3], or a combination[4].

<u>Harvard style referencing</u> is common in the humanities and social sciences, but also widely used in biological sciences. The author and year of publication is noted within the text itself.

> *EXAMPLE: It has been postulated that this system might involve other key components (Jones et al., 2009).*

"Et al." is an abbreviation of *et alii*, which is Latin for "and others," and may be used for multiple author articles.

Referring to an **author point of view** can be made similarly for both Vancouver and Harvard style.

> *EXAMPLES:*
> *Jones (1991) considered this a critical consideration for the field.*
> *Jones[1] considered this a critical consideration for the field.*

You can also refer to **specific page numbers** in your referencing.

> *EXAMPLES:*
> *Smith et al. (4, p.43) considered this a critical consideration for the field.*
> *Smith et al. (2010, p.43) considered this a critical consideration for the field.*

Further advice and guidance on referencing styles is abundantly available, and for journal articles you should follow the instructions to authors provided by your target journal. Some recommended texts include:

1: Neville, C. (2010). The Complete Guide to Referencing and Avoiding Plagiarism. 2nd Edn. Open University Press. ISBN-10:0335241034.

2: Lipson, C. (2011). Cite Right. A Quick Guide to Citation Styles- MLA, APA, Chicago, the Sciences, Professions, and More. 2nd Edn. The University of Chicago Press. ISBN-10: 0226484645.

3: Pears, R. and Shields, G. (2016). Cite Them Right. The Essential Referencing Guide. 10th Edition. Palgrave. ISBN: 9781137585042.

Appendices

You may include a range of content in your appendices to complement the main study that you are presenting and to provide clarity for your dissertation. This might include any of the following matter.

Full ethics approvals: Most institutions will advise that you include an outline of your ethics approvals in the statement of originality (preliminary pages), where you provide the clearance numbers and brief details of what they are clearing you for. You may wish to also include your full ethics approvals in your appendices as a reference for the study.

Safety approvals: You may include safety approvals in full to complement those outlined in the statement of originality (preliminary pages).

Questionnaires/Surveys: If you have utilized questionnaires or surveys as part of your thesis investigations but these have not been included in the original publications, you may choose to include them in the appendices as reference material.

Technical details of the work/analysis: You may include further clarification of particularly technical aspects of the work in the appendices so that the reader can better perceive the work that you are presenting. Some examples of what you might outline here in detail include:
- Genotyping strategies.
- Equipment characteristics.
- Breeding or surveying structure.

Supplementary material: This is typically included in the chapters specific to the articles themselves, because the journal article and its supplementary material represents the entire study presented. Some institutions may, however, request that supplementary material is included in the appendices.

Related published content: You may choose to include relevant content that you have published and which is not considered a central thesis publication. This might include:
- NCBI published sequences.
- Articles/papers that may be relevant to the overall thesis, such as content you published leading to your doctoral work.
- Guidelines that frame your investigation.

END OF CHAPTER 7 SUMMARY
Discussion, References, and Appendices

Here I have discussed concerns relating to the discussion, conclusions, references, and appendices sections, which draw together the overall thesis findings and clarify their contribution to the field. Some key concerns were covered, including:

- The main goal of the discussion is to frame the overall study findings in relation to the current state of the art of the field.

- You may choose to include figures or diagrams in this section to clarify your contributions to the field.

- You should relate the findings from each chapter to each other, referring to each by their Roman numeral as assigned in the list of publications.

- The discussion may be presented, at least in part, as a published review.

- References should be provided to support the content presented around the articles, but the articles typically carry internal chapter-specific references.

- A range of content may be included in the appendices to provide reference material for the overall investigation.

EXERCISE 7.1: SUMMARIZE MAJOR FINDINGS
Outline the major findings of your investigation using bullet points. Once you have established this list, creatively arrange the content to form a logical reflective narrative.

References — chapter 7
Rowland, J.E. (2003) Trangenic analysis of Growth Hormone Receptor intracellular signaling pathways. *University of Queensland doctoral dissertation.*

CHAPTER 8

Tying it all Together

In this section, I consider some of the final concerns that you might address in presenting your overall thesis by publication, including submission and follow-up.

Cover Design

The size and style of your final printed thesis will depend on your university guidelines, but all theses will have a front and back cover. For some, the back cover is negligible, but others are presented in a style similar to a paperback book. In both cases, you will often require a standard thesis title for the front cover and a short title for the spine (also usable as a header). This differs from the title page discussed in chapter 3.

Running titles

Short running titles for each of your articles are often requested for the purpose of publishing the original manuscript. Similarly, the running title (often 60 characters or less) for the thesis will be able to be used on the spine of the thesis, and in the headers and footers.

Some examples from published theses include the following.

> Long title: Transgenic mouse models of growth hormone receptor signaling.
>
> Short title: Growth hormone receptor signaling.

Reference: Rowland, J.E. (2013). Transgenic mouse models of growth hormone receptor signaling *in vivo*. University of Queensland.

Long title: The effect of environmental conditions on the nature and detection of volcanic clouds.

Potential short title: Environment and volcanic clouds.

Reference: Tupper, A. (2007). The effect of environmental conditions on the nature and detection of volcanic clouds. Monash School of Mathematical Science.

Long title: The role of the neuropeptide Y system on B cell development and function.

Short title: Neuropeptide Y and B Cells.

Reference: Geetha, R. (2010). The role of the neuropeptide Y system on B cell development and function. University of New South Wales, Clinical School – St Vincent's Hospital.

Final Format Polishing

When you reach the stage that your thesis master document is set up and the papers inserted accordingly, you need to complete some final formatting to ensure it is ready to print or publish digitally. You should also have friends or colleagues assist you to review these issues in tandem, because by this stage of your thesis preparation you will probably stop noticing mistakes because you are too embedded in the process. A fresh pair of eyes is always helpful. Here is a list of some major points to address in a final format polishing review.

To do list:
- Headers and footers.
- Polish your references.

- Check tables and figures.
- Check page numbers.
- Check pagination and clean layout throughout.
- Proof the language for spelling and style.
- Proof the entire manuscript for errors (content/layout).

Each of these are discussed in more detail in this section.

Headers and footers

Headers and footers provide a guide for your reader to easily identify the section and focus of the work that they are currently reading. Classically, these will include one or more of the following:
- Short thesis title.
- Section heading.
- Author name.
- Short publication title.

Polishing your headers and footers is one of the final formatting tasks that you will need to perform.

Polish your references

Before you send your thesis for assessment, you should absolutely complete a final reference check. In this process, you should check two main concerns.

1) **Accuracy** of the referencing must be confirmed: that you have referenced the correct papers in the right location, and ensured that the reference details match (number/paper; author/paper).

2) **Formatting** of the referencing must be checked: style of referencing must be consistent.

Tables and figures

You must check your tables and figures for numbering and errors in your final revision of the document. In particular, you may have images that you have inserted as pictures that carry text, which can be **formatted poorly, be of too-low resolution, or carry spelling mistakes**. This happens quite often and is a major issue I have confronted as an academic editor. Table and figure **numbering errors** are also very common; you may have repeated or skipped numbers, making it challenging for the reader to follow your presentation of the study.

When preparing figures and tables, it is imperative that you maintain a **consistent style**. In the sections surrounding the journal articles, an elegant thesis will present matching tables and figures that follow a standard format. The format should render the interpretation of your content to be simple and easy to follow. Make sure that you take time to review your tables and figures after you have drafted your thesis and before submitting.

Numbering

As outlined in chapter 2, you must **standardize your numbering** in your dissertation. Ensure that you are using uniform styles of numbering for pages, figures and tables, papers, and section numbers in your dissertation, and double check that this has been done systematically once you complete your manuscript. Cross reference your tables and figures to ensure that they follow clear numerical flow throughout the manuscript, and ensure that they match the list of tables and list of figures.

Page numbering can become messed up when you are formatting your manuscript in different sections, or inserting pages from elsewhere in the final stages of preparation. Be sure to carefully check the page numbering of your manuscript and ensure that it conforms with the numbers noted in your final table of contents, list of tables, and list of figures.

Layout and format

You should complete a final check that your **gutters**, **margins**, and **fonts** are consistent throughout your dissertation. Pay attention to font restrictions when setting up your document and be sure to edit and revise your manuscript. This must be checked again once you have put your whole manuscript together, because strange formatting can often result from late changes to your work.

You may be using mirrored margins, multiple sections, or varied formatting in different parts of your thesis manuscript, thus overall page layout should be checked prior to submitting. Complete a final check that you meet all the requirements for layout that are defined by your institution. Guidelines may have changed since you last noted the layout requirements for your work.

Editing/Proofing

Editing and proofreading are the two most important things to do in the final stages before printing, and you must be sure to allow yourself time to do these before submitting your thesis to print or digital publication. Spelling and grammar checkers are useful but not perfect. If you have time at this stage to have others read the manuscript, it is advisable. If you have the money, and particularly if you are not confident in your writing skills, paying a professional editor to review your manuscript is also recommended. It is important to petition a qualified editor who only makes language corrections/line editing, and does not impact the content. You are being assessed for your delivery of your own ideas, and these must be retained when you are submitting your work for examiner review.

Top tips to polish your writing

1: Review and revise.

2: Get a proofreader from your discipline.

This might be another member of your research group who is interested in your work, or a colleague from your institution.

3: Get an editor.

A contentious issue with the use of academic editors is that you may be assumed to have a higher level of English skills if you submit a very well written dissertation. It is thus important that you **acknowledge any editing and revision** that you have had done on your thesis. As for all aspects of the thesis, clear communication of this information within the text is important.

ISBN

Some universities will request that you include an ISBN number when you submit your dissertation. This may be provided by your institution, or you may choose to acquire your own. Indeed, if your institution requires you to use an ISBN, they will likely have a system in place to issue you with one prior to you publishing your dissertation. Some universities may require two ISBN numbers: one for your print version, and another for your digital version. You should have investigated the requirements for an ISBN by the time you draft your thesis by publication.

Very few theses by publication are later published as book titles, given that most of the work has already been presented as published articles. If you wish to later publish your work as a marketable book title, you may later acquire an ISBN to make your title more widely sellable/available.

Exemplars

Most universities will advise you to **look at example theses in your field** when it comes time to tie your work together. Reviewing others' approaches to drafting a thesis can give you good ideas, and these will likely derive from more than one source. I always advise my students to find exemplars of the style of writing that they need to deliver, should they be writing content for any particular publication target. This advice usually relates to the production of journal articles, but theses are no less valid for this approach. You will gain valuable ideas about how you want to present and deliver your thesis by publication by reviewing a range of completed theses in your discipline, and in others.

A Word on Writing ...

If you're pursuing any kind of academic research, you need to build your communication skillset. If you fail to communicate the work, what is the point of pursuing it? Whether it be for report, journal article, thesis, abstract, or grant writing, you need to communicate your work in written form. If you wish to do this well, I advise you to build a writing practice from the very beginning of your time as a researcher. You may feel that this is an abstract concept, particularly if your research is experimentally focused. However, I put forward the following concepts of the different types of writing that you might pursue during different stages of the project.

Literature review

You should always maintain an up-to-date perspective on the state of the art in your discipline. Regularly reading journal articles, adding them to your reference manager, and building your literature review as you pursue your studies is critical to staying on top of your discipline and potential advancements you can incorporate in your research. Take time to set up your literature review at the commencement of your candidature, and systematically build on your review as you progress through your research. Set some time aside each week to build a regular practice in this regard, which will carry you through your academic career.

Methods
It is advisable to keep your methodology records up to date as you proceed through your investigation. If you consistently maintain your methods throughout your doctoral studies, you will have a minimum amount of work to do when it comes time to draft your research articles or the methodology section of your thesis, if you choose to include one.

Abstract
The abstract is usually the last thing that you write for your thesis by publication, and indeed for each journal article that you submit. When drafting an abstract, you need to consider the whole document that you are presenting; you need to outline the overall study and how it progresses, so that it is an overview for your reader.

Discussion/Conclusions
You should be considering the major points that you will include in your thesis throughout your candidature. Creating a list of points to include in your final conclusions should be an ongoing activity for you throughout your doctoral studies, after you commence your data collection. Keeping a notebook always handy is a great way to capture those lightbulb moment ideas that can greatly deepen your reflection on the relevance of your work, which should be demonstrated clearly in your discussion and conclusions. Similarly, you might tinker with ideas for graphical ways to demonstrate your overall findings, and to demonstrate how the articles that constitute your results chapters fit together. Keeping your ideas in a notebook or diary, or even a rough collection of paper collated together, will simplify your thesis writing immensely.

Reports
While pursuing your doctoral studies, it would be wise to arrange regular progress reports with your supervisor/mentor in order to keep everyone up to date with your project progress. These provide

checkpoints for you to reflect on your work and its significance, which can provide content that you can include in your thesis when it comes time to draft the manuscript. Reports may be structured with method summaries, logical explanations of the recent stages of your work, recent results, short conclusions, and explanations regarding the next stage of the work.

Journal articles
Journal article drafting should be your main writing focus as you progress through your doctorate if you are aiming to present a thesis by publication. The process by which you build your journal articles will typically commence with your development of a clear results section, coupled with methods; but even before commencing your research investigations, you should have a clear background review prepared, which can drive your investigation. The final material to put together for your article should encompass the discussion and abstract, in order to reflect on the individual study outcomes.

Grant/funding applications
If you are attending a university that offers competitive funding applications for research students, you have an opportunity to develop your capacity to market your research to source resources for your professional/research advancement. Like many students, you will probably need to source ongoing funding throughout your candidature to fund your livelihood, and you will do this through scholarship applications to various organizations or initiatives. Strategy for sourcing funding is a topic that will be discussed to a greater extent in later titles, but developing your skills to be able to market yourself for funding is certainly a critical component of becoming a successful researcher, and is worth pursuing. Any reflective practice that encourages you to think about your research from a novel perspective, thus persuasively communicate your work, is warranted.

Acknowledgements
Various approaches may be taken to drafting your acknowledgements. You might either commence writing this section as you begin your degree and update throughout (my personal approach), or reflect on your whole experience immediately before submitting. I recommend you allow some time for drafting this section, because everyone that reads your dissertation will read this section to gauge who you are as a person.

Structuring the manuscript
You should structure out your thesis manuscript in the first six months of your PhD, so you have a perspective on the content that you are striving to prepare in the course of delivering a thesis by publication. This approach will give you time to develop your thesis layout and presentation as you progress (see chapter 2).

Curriculum Vitae (C.V.)
When it comes close to the time that you will be completing your doctoral studies, in your final year of your PhD you will likely be looking at your next professional position. During this time, it is worth your while to consider how you will structure your curriculum vitae for various targets, as well as considering your next professional direction. In fact, it is worth taking time throughout your studies to consider the path that you wish to take professionally after your PhD. In the current education system, we produce more doctoral graduates than there are research positions, and you may find yourself a perennial postdoc if you fail to plan your career well. Maintaining an up-to-date C.V. tailored for the professional direction that you wish to take will aid your professional advancement in the direction of your choosing. At the very least, it will be on hand for when opportunities arise, be those for funding or collaborating, or for professional roles.

Cover letters

You will need to be able to draft well-crafted and strategic cover letters or emails for various reasons throughout your doctoral studies. For instance, you may be contacting potential collaborators for resources that you need to progress your work; you may be applying for funding, in which case a summary of your strengths and reasoning for your competitiveness needs to be clarified; you may be submitting an abstract or article for consideration to attend a conference; or you may be writing the cover letter for your research article to be submitted to a peer reviewed journal.

<u>Summary of Major Writing Foci</u>

- THESIS
    - Acknowledgements
    - Literature review
    - Methods
    - Abstract
    - Discussion/Conclusions
- Reports
- Journal articles
- Grant/funding applications
- Manuscript structure
- Curriculum vitae
- Cover letters

Final Submission

When you have completed your thesis drafting and the entire manuscript is ready for submission, you must ensure that you have clarity on the submission requirements as well as any final paperwork that is required before you graduate.

Submission format:
Some theses are submitted electronically for review, and some institutions require paper versions. This is something you should have identified earlier in your candidature, but ensure now that you have the correct format for your submission, prior to sending.

Final Reports and Paperwork
It is important that you submit your final paperwork and reports to ensure that you will be able to graduate once your thesis is finalized. Clarify report requirements, which may cover end-of-candidature, funding-body, or departmental requirements, for example.

Update Records and Clarify Contacts
Depending on your institution, you may be granted a grace period where you retain your institutional email and access whilst you await your thesis revision. Be sure to update your contact details and clarify your institutional access with administrative staff around the time that you are required to submit your thesis. This can reduce stress when it comes time to address your revisions, if any.

Responses to Examiners
After you have received your feedback from examiners, you may receive a range of requests, which you can respond to in various ways. How you respond may relate to whether the examiner is querying published papers or original data chapters.

If you present your published chapters in the same format as your thesis, rather than that of the journal it was published in, you may receive more requests to modify the paper itself than you might otherwise have dealt with. There are ways that you can address requests to modify already published papers. Thus, here I present some approaches you might take in responding to examiners for both unpublished, and published sections of your thesis. I focus on three common requests, whereby actual changes to the thesis contents are required, rather than simple answers to queries: additional data, grammatical corrections, and further justification.

Additional Data
If your examiner requests additional data to be amended to your thesis, and this is practical for you to do so, you may easily amend this data to unpublished sections of your thesis. You should note this accordingly in your response to the examiner.

> *"The dataset requested has been assessed and amended to Chapter 4, page 92, of the thesis"*

If this additional data is requested for the published article, you may go about it in two ways.

1. You may amend it to the article if you have included the article to your thesis in thesis-style format. That is, not in the format that it was published in the journal. If you take this approach, you must make an addendum, specific to the thesis, outlining the changes that have been included after the work was published. The addendum should be noted in the pages surrounding the manuscript in the chapter where it is presented.

   EXAMPLE:
   Addendum: Additional triplicate data points for 12, 24, and 48 hours have been amended to figure 5 after publication in [journal name]. These changes are included specifically for this thesis.

   As such, in your response to the examiner, you may write:

   > *"The dataset requested has been collected and added to figure 5 in study I, with an addendum noting the change on page 92 of the thesis."*

Changes may be amended to your published articles after your thesis has been sent to the examiners. Changes are often published as an **addendum** in the journal. A published addendum may be included to the chapter with a note to the examiners after revision.

"An addendum to this article was published whilst the thesis was under examination. It is now included to chapter 4, following the original article"

2. You may include additional data as an extra section within the chapter after the paper itself. This is more appropriate where the paper is presented in the journal-style format. If the article itself is unchanged, no further addendum is required.

<u>EXAMPLE:</u>
4.2   Additional Results
Additional data sets relevant to this paper, which were collected after publication, are included here…

In this case, in your response to the examiner, you may write:

"The dataset requested has been collected and included to a new section, 4.2, appearing immediately following the manuscript to which it is relevant."

<u>Grammatical Corrections</u>
Grammatical corrections may be easily included to most sections of the thesis, but if the examiner notes grammatical changes for your published articles, you may still include the changes, ensuring that you indicate this in the results chapter as a note. For instance:

In this thesis, some minor grammatical changes have been included to the manuscript after publication in [journal name].

In this case, you may respond to your examiner with an explanation of how you had incorporated the grammatical changes:

> *"The grammatical changes requested have been incorporated to article 1."*

However, in some cases you may not be able to incorporate grammatical changes to the published article, in which case you might respond to your reviewer in an alternative fashion:

> *"Given that the article noted has been peer reviewed and published, the grammatical changes requested have not been incorporated to the article itself. Nonetheless, the pages surrounding the published paper have been corrected accordingly."*

<u>Further Justification/Explanation</u>
Your examiner might request that you further expand your discussion of the data that you presented in your papers. In this case, they may request that you include a wider collection of reference materials to provide a greater depth to your interpretation of the results. In this scenario, for unpublished work, modifications may usually be incorporated to the current chapter's discussion section, and further references added accordingly. However, for published papers, you might add further discussion in the pages following the paper itself. Alternatively, the extended discussion requested might be best added to the final discussion chapter that overviews the entire study.

Your response to the examiner might be addressed as follows:

> *"Given that the article noted has been peer reviewed and published, the expanded discussion requested has not been incorporated to the article itself. An extended discussion has been included following the presentation of the article within chapter 4, as well as in the final discussion in chapter 9. The suggested references have been included to the bibliography in chapter 10."*

END OF CHAPTER 8 SUMMARY
Tying it all Together

This chapter has covered the final considerations that should be taken as you tie together the overall thesis manuscript. These considerations include the following:

- You must consider the design of your final dissertation prior to printing.

- Major foci should be polished prior to submitting/printing, including:
    - headers/footers
    - references
    - tables and figures
    - pagination and page numbers

- We review the major writing foci during candidature

- You may include an ISBN for your thesis.

- Exemplars should be employed to guide you in your thesis preparation.

- Ensure that you complete all of the official documentation and follow the key guidelines when it comes time to submit your thesis.

- We review common responses to examiner's requests.

EXERCISE 8.1: CHECKLIST FOR SUBMISSION

Create a checklist of all of the final tasks and checks required prior to submitting your dissertation. This may include specific sections you wish to polish, page checks, numbering, consistency, headers/footers, or overall style. Include deadlines for each task, with realistic expectations for how long you will need to complete your preparation.

SUMMARY

Thank you for reading through this entire book, where we have explored the different technical aspects associated with delivering a thesis by publication. We have covered the essential planning stages for your research, and the delivery of each section of the thesis. The content was presented in eight chapters in the following order:

- Chapters 1 and 2 covered the planning and practical approaches that you might consider in pursuing your doctoral investigations that will ultimately lead to a thesis by publication.

- Chapter 3 outlined the type of content that you might include to the preliminary pages, framing your thesis presentation.

- Chapter 4 discussed considerations of how to deliver your literature review which leads to your overall research aims.

- Chapter 5 presented the kind of content that you might include to a methods section in the thesis by publication.

- Chapter 6 focused on the structure of the chapters that present your research papers.

- Chapter 7 delineated the approach you might take in drawing your study together into one cohesive discussion, as well as references and appendices.

- Chapter 8 covered the final matters you need to manage in preparing to submit your dissertation for review.

Taken together, these chapters provide you with a concise overview of the materials that you need to create to deliver a clear and logical thesis by publication.

I hope that you have found this guide useful, as the second title published in the Practical Academic series of books designed to support research academics internationally. I encourage you to provide feedback in the contact form on the website (www.practicalacademic.com) or via other non-biased online feedback platforms. If this book has helped you in any way, I'd like to know how, and what aspects of the material most supported you. Similarly, if you felt it could be improved upon, please do let me know, so that I can improve the material in later titles and editions.

With thanks and warm regards,

Jennifer Rowland

If you enjoyed this title, you might like to read "Practical Academic: Managing Research Groups and Projects."

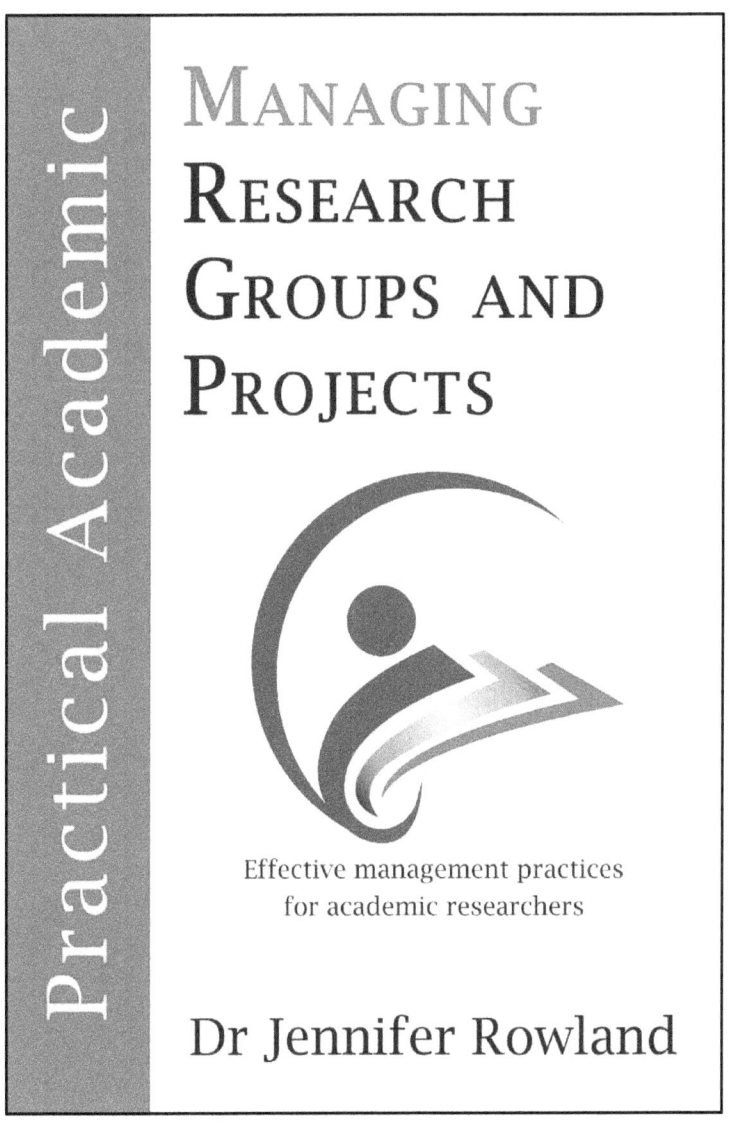

It is available as a paperback from Amazon or the Book Depository, and as a Kindle e-book.

INDEX

Abbreviations 49, 50, 53, 54, 93
Abstract 26, 33, 50-54, 76, 104-108
Acknowledgements 5, 26, 33, 43-49, 54-55, 107-108, 118
Addendum 110-111
Additional data 110-111
Aims 26, 33, 56-57, 62-65, 84-85
Appendices 26, 33, 42, 85-88, 94-96
Arxiv 76
Attendance – conferences/seminars 16

Backing up 29, 30, 34

Conference proceeding 5, 72-77
Collation of data 38, 58
Contributions list 43
Copyright 37
Corrections 102, 110-111
Cover design 98
Cover letters 108
Cotutelle 30, 32
Curriculum Vitae (C.V.) 107-108

Database of resources 18
Data
    additional 110-111
    analysis 19
    collation 38, 58
    collection 45
    loss 29
    presentation 59, 67, 74, 109
    supplementary 76
Deadlines 16, 19-20, 29, 114
Deliverables 9, 12, 16

Digital theses 28
Discussion 85, 88-92, 96, 105-108, 112-115

Earlier studies 70, 82
Editing 102-103
Ethics 37-38, 94-96
Examination 102
    time 29, 34
    response 109-113
    requests 109-113
    selection of examiner 29, 34
    acknowledgement of examiner 46, 53-54
Exemplars 103-104, 113

Fakery 78
Figures 33, 39-40, 53-54, 58-60, 71, 88-90, 96, 100-101, 113
Financial support 16
Font 28, 102
Footers 98-100, 113-114
Foreign Language Articles 75
Format
    journal article 72-74, 79, 111
    numbering 101
    references 92, 100
    table of contents 39
    tables and figures 58, 71, 101
    thesis 26-28, 32, 75, 79, 99-102, 109-110
    title page 36

GANNT 9
Grants 47, 104, 106
Grammatical corrections 110-112

Headers 25, 98-100, 113-114

Hours of work 14

Institutional services 18, 20
Introduction 26, 33, 52, 56-58, 65, 80-87
ISBN 103, 113

Joint thesis 30, 32
Journal
      article 57, 69-70, 99, 104-108
      contributors 43-45
      format 72-74, 79-80, 111
      language 27, 75
      target journal 19, 26, 73-77, 94
      permission/copyright 30, 37, 77, 82, 84
      publication status 42, 73-77
      supplementary material 66, 76, 95

Language 27, 47, 75, 100, 102
Layout of manuscript 25-28, 33-34, 65, 75, 100, 102, 107
List of Contributors 25, 33, 41-46, 53-54, 84
List of Figures 39-40, 53-54
List of Original Publications 25, 33, 40-43, 53-54, 57, 73, 83, 95
List of Tables 39-40, 53-54, 101
Literature Review 33, 56-59, 65, 82-85, 104, 108, 115

Margins 28, 102
Meetings schedule 15, 119
Mentoring checklist 13-15, 24
Methods 33, 39, 66-71, 84-85, 105-108, 115
Microdeliverables 9
Mixed results chapters 75
Multiple authors 83

Note keeping 89

Numerics 27, 100-101

Open access 77-78
Ownership 18
Oxford comma 25

Page numbers 35, 80, 93, 100-101, 113
Peer review 6, 76-78, 108, 112
Permissions 30-34, 37, 41, 58, 73-75, 79-86
Planning 8-26, 32, 45, 72-73, 115
Practical preparation 25-34
Predatory publishers 77-79
Preliminary pages 30, 35-57, 74, 83-85, 94
Prepared journal article 42, 74-75, 106
Printing and binding 18, 28, 32, 34, 79, 102, 113
Proofing 100-102
Publication status 43, 73-77
Publishing platforms 75-77

Record keeping 18
Referencing 26-28, 33, 37, 59, 75, 83-88, 92-96
Repetition 57, 82, 84
Reports 104-110
Results 72-87
Running title 98

Safety 38, 94
Section numbers 27, 101
Sherpa RoMEO 77
SMART planning 12, 20
Spacing 27, 49
Spamming 78
SSRN 76
Statement of Originality 25, 30, 33, 37-38

Structuring 107
Summary table 59, 60
Supervisor
    acknowledgment 46, 53-54
    relationship 8-20, 30, 42-47, 53-55, 77, 105
Supplementary material 66, 76, 95

Tables 40, 58-59, 65, 71, 100-101, 113
Table of Contents 39, 53-54, 80, 101
Title Page 9, 25, 30-36, 53-54, 98
Traditional theses 5-8, 36, 56-57, 65, 70-75

www.ingramcontent.com/pod-product-compliance
Lightning Source LLC
Chambersburg PA
CBHW072054290426
44110CB00014B/1680